# Levelling Up
## Good Governance and Effective Planning

# Levelling Up
## Good Governance and Effective Planning


Roger Read

**Disclaimer**

Statements of fact and opinion in the articles in *Levelling Up* are those of the author. College Publications does not make any representation, express or implied, in respect of the accuracy of the material in this book and cannot accept any legal responsibility or liability for any errors or omissions that may be made. The reader should make his/her own evaluation as to the appropriateness or otherwise of any experimental technique described.

ISBN 978-1-84890-364-7


College Publications
Scientific Director: Dov Gabbay
Managing Director: Jane Spurr


http://www.collegepublications.co.uk


Original cover design by Laraine Welch

# Introduction

## Levelling Up

Across Europe there has been a general widening of disparities between citizens, communities and regions. There comes a point where these threaten the social cohesion of nation states, with adverse effects on their prosperity and wellbeing. This has been recognised by the European Union through its social and economic programmes to address deprivation and by nation states through social, economic and environmental policies designed to promote "Levelling Up" and address disadvantages.

This book presents the case for Good Governance and Effective Planning as a means through which to achieve Levelling Up. In summary.

- Recognise that Subsidiarity needs to be accepted as the basic principle for Good Governance. It means decisions being taken at the level to which they apply. National, regional and community.

- Recognise that regions, and in particular metropolitan or city regions, need to be the key building blocks for good governance.

- Give them statutory powers over the key functions that need to be integrated, for example, strategic planning (Including climate change, centres, housing and retailing), transportation, economic development, social services, health, education, police (security), water and sewerage and environmental safeguarding and recovery.

- Require them to produce and cost a Regional Report identifying the key regional issues, problems and opportunities, that need to be addressed and the decisions and actions required for effective responses. And to then monitor and roll these forward on a regular basis.

- Enable them to negotiate the required levels of short and longer-term finance from local funding and central government levelling up support.

# Good Governance and Effective Planning

## A synoptic guide to the future

Does not every society need a group of people who can look ahead on its behalf? Who are not only well informed about, and understand, the present but who can also present choices for the future? Who can distinguish between the probable and the possible? And who can present the probable as forecasts and the possible as scenarios and visions? They have been likened to the navigators on a voyage, responding to changing circumstances but always keeping destinations in view. Their sole influence is informed argument and an ability to research the knowledge they need for this. But knowledge, of itself, is not enough. What is also needed is real understanding and insight. How is society working and changing and how can the change in prospect be presented as choices for the future? Are these inevitable or can they be influenced? In the public interest and the common good. This is planning and it is the lost dimension to public affairs. We need it back for the wellbeing of us all.

Roger Read.

October 2021.

*"To plan is a basic human need" - Patrick Geddes 1854-1932. Scottish biologist, sociologist, geographer and town planner who pioneered the concept of the "synoptic (all embracing) view" of regions.*

# Good Governance and Effective Planning

## Subsidiarity

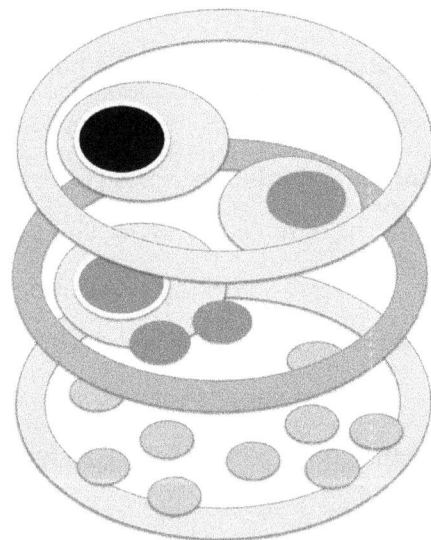

**National governance**
*Context and National Frameworks*

**Regional and Metropolitan**
governance
*Strategies*
*Policies and Programmes*

**Local and Community governance**
*Plans and proposals*

*See Tables on pages 21 and 22 for more detail.*

# Themes and contents

- **What happened? – How planning lost its way**
- Subsidiarity – Who does what?

- **The big forces for change - The wider context**
- Global warming and environmental impact - Migration and biodiversity
- The world post COVID 19 – How change became essential
- Globalisation and automation - The future of work
- The financialisation of everything - Development as an asset

- **What needs planning? – The really important issues**
- The synoptic view – How the pieces fit together
- Foresight – Taking the long view
- Subsidiarity – Who plans what?
- The Metropolitan dimension – Where it all happens

- **What might better look like?**
- Exemplars – Europe does it better
- We need planners - Educating the planners
- The Planning profession - The need for a voice
- Communitaire – The politics of basic human needs
- How to make it happen – Who needs to do what?

# What happened? – How planning lost its way

## Centralisation

Subsidiarity is the awkward word used to describe the idea that decisions should be taken at the level to which they apply. So, for example, that central government should not be involved in decisions about local housing, health or education needs and development. But the level at which decisions in the public interest are taken is also related to where the financial resources lie and whether local taxation meets all local needs. Some regions and localities will be more prosperous than others and central taxes enable the equalisation of financial resources to all. However, this process can lead to the centralisation of decision making where central government wants to decide both the financial support needed and how and where it should be spent.

So subsidiarity is intimately related to governance and the tiers of governance that a country adopts to manage its affairs and public finances. As was explained in the preceding foreword, effective planning is required at all levels of governance to ensure that strategic visions are realised and also that local needs are met. Centralisation

1

seeks to ensure that the control of implementation is retained but this often means that success will be limited through a lack of compliance and "buy in". Only by persuading all levels of governance to support a vision and its related strategies, through reasoned argument, can central government achieve it aims. It cannot achieve everything itself nor should it try to do so.

Effective planning has been a victim of centralisation where governance at the regional and local levels is simply the implementation arm of central government, with little autonomy of its own. Central government has used proxies, such as boards or agencies, to localise its control but these also disenfranchise citizens from decisions that affect their wellbeing and futures. Effective planning, at all levels of governance, based on the concept of subsidiarity, is one way of ensuring that needs are identified and met and opportunities are identified and realised.

To the extent that governance has lost its way so the role of planning has diminished as well, for example, to local spatial planning and development control. By advocating regional and metropolitan (a city region and its area of influence) governance planning can begin to re-establish its critical enabling role at these levels.

## Loss of regional and local autonomy

The critical levels of governance below the national are the regional and metropolitan levels. This is because these are the levels where strategic decisions are required. The subsidiarity test is whether they are "regionally significant" or not. In effect, do they have a regional or metropolitan dimension?

As cities have grown they have developed suburbs and satellite towns and settlements within their areas of influence. These look to the core city for higher-level health, education, retailing, leisure and employment opportunities. They become "polycentric". The necessary transport infrastructure has to be provided together with strategic utility (water, sewerage and energy etc.) networks. Locations for growth have to be identified (Greenfield development) whilst making the most of locations within urban areas (Brownfield development). Valued environmental resources have to be safeguarded. All of this requires integrated strategic planning in the wider public interest.

Regional and metropolitan authorities need to be in place to manage this process if incoherent sprawl is to be avoided and integrated strategic planning is to be able to contribute its benefits effectively. Regional autonomy is a necessity for effective planning, the provision

3

of coherent strategies and a context within which local authorities can then exercise their autonomy with confidence.

## Monopolies

In a market economy business tends to absorb competitors up to the point where government regards choice as having been compromised. Countries have competition authorities to regulate this. Nevertheless, in areas such as retailing and house building, the result has been a limited number of very large operators with considerable influence and power. They have the financial capability to invest and speculate in locations for development and to press their proposals through the planning appeal process.

Strategic planning has to be in a position to play a proactive role in identifying needs and the spatial planning opportunities to meet them, which requires, for example, an understanding of regional housing market areas and regional retail catchment areas. Only under the umbrella of regional strategies for housing and retailing can local planning direct speculative development pressures by large-scale operators and developers to locations that are in the wider public interest. For example, to locations with good accessibility by public transport, that can be integrated with existing urban communities and

4

do not have an unacceptable environmental impact. In most cases this will mean Brownfield rather than Greenfield locations.

Where effective regional and metropolitan planning does not exist, or local plans are not up to date, then local planning is left exposed to the pressures of monopolistic speculation and outcomes that are not in the public interest. Monopolies are powerful advocates of their own interests and equally strong strategic planning, based on reasoned argument, is required to safeguard the public interest.

## Planning as enabler rather than controller

There is a perception that planning, as a public interest function, is more concerned with controlling rather than enabling. The two functions are inter-related. For example, in its enabling role planning can identify opportunities for development that maximise benefits and minimise adverse impacts. It can bring these to the market and promote them. It can then control adverse proposals by offering better alternatives.

However, such positive planning can only take place within a governance structure that requires the integrated production and regular updating of plans, policies and proposals, at all levels. It has

5

to be proactive rather than reactive. In this way planning will be seen, by politicians and the public, as a force for good and valued accordingly.

## Short term versus long term - The electoral cycle

However, there is a recurring difficulty, which is the short-term uncertainties of the electoral cycle that can mitigate against confidence in the longer-term view taken in regional and metropolitan strategies. This is why it will always be important that longer-term strategies are well founded in reasoned argument and command wide recognition and acceptance.

Elections can take place at varying times at national, regional, metropolitan and local levels, which leaves strategies and plans open to the possibility of frequent changes in the direction of policy. Planning needs to cope with this through a process of regular review and update to roll strategies and plans forward, to keep ahead of events, and to respond to unforeseen circumstances. Only in this way can planning remain relevant and effective.

# The market for planning - Meeting basic human needs

Planning will always be an important part of the machinery of government that is aimed at identifying and meeting public needs, including those of the market economy, in the most effective way. In a mixed economy, with needs met by both the public and private sectors, for example in housing, caring, education, health and transportation, a distinction can be drawn between need and demand.

Need means meeting basic standards of supply and quality that may be defined and provided by the public sector, for example by a National Health Service, public education system or local authority housing service. It can be quantified and planned for on this basis.

Demand is a function of the market and means making assumptions about the level of basic need being met by the public sector and the scope to go beyond this to offer choice to those fortunate enough to be able to afford it or those who wish to use their disposable income for the consumption of services rather than goods. Planning requires assumptions to be made about such preferences and for these to be open and transparent.

In housing, for example, assumptions will have to be made about tenure choice, that is, between public sector rental, private sector rental and home ownership. Such choices vary markedly across Europe as a result of tradition and affluence and will vary from region to region. They too require transparency about the tenure choice assumptions built in to housing strategies.

In other areas, such as retailing, strategic planning requires assumptions to be made about the use of disposable income for expenditure on convenience (non-durable) and comparison (durable) goods. These are basic human needs met wholly by the market within a framework provided by strategic planning.

So it is clear that strategic planning at the regional and metropolitan levels requires well-informed assumptions about public behaviour in meeting their needs through the public and private sectors and the use of their disposable income. Such assumptions will have to be consistent with the future foreseen for the economy, levels of employment in the public and private sectors and incomes.

These are clearly complex inter relationships that finally result in the provision of land for development (Greenfield) or reuse (Brownfield).

They are integrated decisions that can best be taken at the regional or metropolitan level.

Land uses will be the generators of traffic on the transport network and the need for mobility may, again, be met privately through car usage, cycling or walking, or the public sector, through public transport. Such "modal split" assumptions feed in to transport models for a region or metropolitan area and can influence policies for provision, for example for cycle-ways, or constraint, for example through road charging.

Foreseeing and meeting the need for services, development and accessibility to meet acknowledged human needs through the public and private sectors, in a mixed economy, is a key function of strategic planning at the regional and metropolitan levels. It requires high-level knowledge, information and insight into the realities on human behaviour. As such, strategic planning is a skilled vocation.

## Reasoned justification - Informed decision-making

The bedrock of strategic planning is "reasoned justification". This is the term used in much planning legislation to describe the requirement for all planning, at whatever level, to be "evidence based" and, beyond this, to be able to present rational arguments to substantiate strategies, policies, programmes and proposals. It is the foundation from which planning can provide some consistency and durability in volatile times, politically or socially.

Here automation now provides the technology to store, select and manipulate data quickly and at a large scale. It enables computer modelling to explore alternative futures and their implications and to make informed choices in the full knowledge of any risks or uncertainties. It enables these to be quantified and presented for political consideration and informed decision-making at the regional and metropolitan levels.

These are specialist skills that can be developed most effectively at the regional and metropolitan levels. They can only be acquired through experience in practice and will then be a valuable resource. It will be wise to develop and retain such skills "in house" so that a regional or metropolitan authority has the capability to fulfil its core functions and responsibilities without having to resort to the uncertainties of "out sourcing".

## What happened? – How planning lost its way

Planning lost its way across much of Europe through a combination of government centralisation, the lack of effective levels of regional and metropolitan governance, pressure from monopoly interests that put financial gain before the public interest, the loss of enabling strategic planning leading to perceptions of planning primarily as a local control mechanism and the short term electoral cycle affecting the ability to take a longer term view.

**All of these adverse effects can be addressed through the adoption, with conviction and commitment, of subsidiarity as the guiding principle of governance.**

# Subsidiarity – Who does what?

## Subsidiarity* - The idea of context and a hierarchy of integrated rolling decision making

There are some 272 recognised (Eurostat) metropolitan regions, with populations over 250,000, in Europe. They include some 70% of the population and are the major urban areas of the continent (see Appendix 2). This is the level at which effective governance is required most because it is where strategic decision-making can have greatest effect. It is the level at which most of the key issues affecting urban Europe need to be addressed and resolved.

But these decisions cannot be taken in isolation. They need a national context in terms of climate change, the economy, energy, infrastructure (transportation and strategic utilities), public services, housing and the environment. Ideally they should be able to operate within a National planning Framework, which brings all of such

* See Footnote on page 20

12

considerations into an integrated whole and clearly sets out how National government sees the country evolving (Vision) and how key national issues are to be tackled (Strategies).

Such a Framework should be subject to the same disciplines as other levels of planning such as regular update and review and a rolling longer-term view. It's essential function would be to set the context for planning at all other levels so that they can recognise the direction that the country as a whole intends to take and plan accordingly.

Planning at the local and community level is where strategies become operational, taking into consideration the regional and metropolitan context and local needs.

There will, inevitably, be tensions between national, regional and local priorities and it would be unrealistic to believe that subsidiarity will resolve all of these. However, this is where the discipline of reasoned argument and decision-making comes into play. As national Frameworks, regional Strategies and local Plans are regularly reviewed, updated and rolled forward, realities will emerge and there will be a greater chance of successful planning and outcomes and the recognition of common interests.

The process of updating, reviewing and rolling forward will recognise that issues will have different time horizons. For example, if an economy is undergoing a process of structural change, as many European economies have done that have de-industrialised, then a two year planning cycle may be appropriate and necessary to manage the recycling and reuse of land and buildings. As such a process continues it may be necessary to take a longer-term view of valued natural and heritage resources and to safeguard them for the future.

So subsidiarity will be complicated by the dynamics of change and the need for planning at all levels to respond to short-term needs and reflect longer-term possibilities in an integrated and cohesive way. Well-informed political leadership will be a prerequisite requiring well-founded planning advice. Planning will have to establish this role again.

## Central government - The wider context

Central government is best placed to be well informed about global change, such as the globalisation of the world economy, climate change, energy supply, migration and urbanisation. These are inter-related, for example, as energy use affects climate change and climate change affects migration. Globalisation and migration affect urbanisation. It will be the role of central government to take a view on these external global matters and their inter relationships, be clear about the necessary strategic responses and communicate these to other levels of governance as the context for their decision making.

Central government also has a responsibility to be well informed on internal matters of national significance such as the changing demographic and social structure of the country, the young, families and the aging population, through births and deaths, household formation and internal migration. It also needs to be well informed about the impact of structural economic change on employment. Insight into such social and economic changes will enable central government to recognise where the needs of regions and communities are likely to exceed the resources available to them and which will require national support.

The European Union has made a range of support funds available to regions and communities in the greatest social and economic need and these recognise the nature of "multiple deprivation" where social and economic need coincides with acute urban and environmental decline. Planning for renewal and regeneration to offset and reverse decline is a matter of national significance.

Central government also has a role to play in identifying positive opportunities for new development, for example, through national programmes for transportation (road, rail, aviation and shipping), public services (health, housing and higher education), support for emerging technologies (renewable energy and transportation) and high-level research (medical and artificial intelligence/automation). They will all have implications for employment and the future of work.

All of these matters could be the substance of National planning Frameworks, with a Vision for the future and Strategies and Programmes for specific sectors of social and economic life, to provide the wider context for regional and metropolitan Strategies and Local Plans and proposals. Such Frameworks will be essential to make clear the intention of government to make subsidiarity a reality.

## Regional and Metropolitan government - The planning Strategies

The regional and metropolitan levels are where the strategic decisions can be made to interpret national Frameworks and then provide a context for planning at the local and community levels.

# Levelling Up - Good Governance and Effective Planning

Foremost is the issue of climate change and how urban areas can change from being the primary source of energy use and greenhouse gas emissions to a source of renewable energy generation and a focus for decarbonisation. This will essentially mean eliminating energy waste, through poor insulation of the building stock, and taking advantage of building surfaces for renewable energy generation using the latest solar film and panel technologies. Metropolitan regions have the potential to transform their urban areas to become the green power stations of the future.

Within a wider region there will be opportunities to be identified for wind and solar power farms and offshore wind. Together with their urban generated energy metropolitan regions can reasonably aim to become largely self-sufficient in renewable energy.

Urbanisation and the strategic need for urban extension or urban renewal and regeneration, or both, will be a key strategic issue for metropolitan regions. Extension has been characterised as Greenfield development and renewal and regeneration as the Brownfield redevelopment of land and buildings.

Reuse and recycling will be part of all regional strategies for decarbonisation but the renewal and regeneration of the urban fabric,

17

of land and buildings, will be the aspect that planning can contribute most to. Urban decline is often associated with social and economic problems and a holistic approach to such areas of "multiple deprivation" will be required, involving planning and public services.

Provision for housing, industry, commerce and retailing will require assessments of need or demand and an assessment of the extent to which these can be met in support of a strategy of renewal and regeneration or require urban extension. In making these strategic judgements planning will have regard to the need to support established urban centres, maximise accessibility by public transport and safeguard green networks.

## Local government - The operational plans of local policies and proposals

It is at the local level that national Frameworks and regional Strategies become operational. It is here that locations become reality. Local plans will respond to all the issues covered by national Frameworks and regional Strategies and add the important assessment of local needs and demands. For example, local housing need may involve an element of new build if the existing housing stock requires restructuring and the lowering of densities.

Green networks will be defined and safeguarded and integrated into the metropolitan and regional fabric.

## How subsidiarity makes for good Governance and effective Planning

The following spreadsheets summarise how the concept of subsidiarity could be applied, in an integrated way, to governance at the national, regional and local levels. This conceptualisation demonstrates the feasibility of such an approach. It has the benefit of clarifying responsibilities and expectations at each level and providing a basis for the allocation of resources for planning to ensure that it is effective as an integrated rolling process. From national Frameworks, through regional Strategies to the realities of Local Plans.

## Footnote

Subsidiarity is the principle that decisions should be taken at the level of governance to which they apply. It has been enshrined in the European Treaties to manage the relationship between the European Union and its constituent Nation States and their respective decision-making and implementation powers. It applies equally to the relationships between levels of European governance.

# Subsidiarity - Good Governance

The tiers of Governance            The functions of Governance

**National governance**            **Wider context**

**National planning Frameworks**   Climate change
**Visions and strategies**         Biodiversity
                                   Economic globalisation
                                   Migration
                                   Global transportation

                                   Social and medical research

**Regional and Metropolitan
governance**

**Regional planning Strategies
Policies and Programmes**

**Local and Community
governance**

Local plans
Policies and Proposals

# Effective Planning

### The functions of governance

National context for regional planning

Issues of national significance

Decarbonisation and energy strategies
Structural economic change
Internal and external migration
National transportation netwoks
Public services - Health, education, welfare
and housing strategies
National environmental safeguarding
National and Regional Parks and tourism
Costal routes and long distance footpaths
Marine nature reserves and fish farming

Regional context for local planning

Issues of regional significance

Decarbonisation and renewable energy provision
Urbanisation (brownfield/greenfield)
Renewal and regeneration priorities
Housing, industry, commerce and
retailing need, demand and provision
Public service provision
Centres
Regional transportation networks
Regional green networks
Regional environmental safeguarding
Infrastructure

Local context for development

Issues of local significance

Decarbonisation and renewable energy locations
Renewal and regeneration locations
Housing, industry, commerce and
retailing provision and locations
Public service provision and locations
Centres
Local transportation networks
Local green networks
Local environmental safeguarding

## Complexity – Defining Regions

Eurostat has used commuting as a measure of the area of influence of the urban core of a region. It concludes that a level of 60% of those in employment commuting to the urban core is a reasonable indicator of its area of influence and also of dependence on the centre for many higher level services such as education, health, retailing and entertainment.

It has used a regional population level of 250,000 as a further indicator to define a "metropolitan" region, that is, one that faces common strategic issues such as transportation networks, housing markets and retail catchment areas. In effect, has a "metropolitan dimension" to its affairs.

Complexity arises with the size and significance of the urban core and its area of influence. For example, in a "polycentric" region, with a number of similar urban cores, areas of influence will overlap. The areas of influence of capital cities, of international or national significance, will overlap with adjoining metropolitan regions. Some regions with primarily rural populations, and a number of smaller towns, may look to an adjoining metropolitan region for the higher level services they need.

Such considerations as these complicate the simple concept of subsidiarity. A capital or metropolitan urban core may provide services beyond its area of influence, in terms of commuting, to a wider rural area that, although taking its own decisions on local and community issues, has needs that can only be met at a regional level.

Good governance and effective planning needs to be aware of, and informed about, such complexities when applying the concept of subsidiarity.

# The big forces for change – The wider context

## Global warming and environmental impact

The Intergovernmental Panel on Climate Change (IPCC) advises the world on climate change and its implications and the choices for adaptation and mitigation. It is in the process of producing eight Reports over the period 2015 to 2023 and the Sixth Assessment Report (AR6) will be completed in 2022.

The first instalment of AR6, released in August 2021, concludes that climate change is affecting rainfall patterns, continuing sea level rises, amplifying the melting of glaciers and ice sheets and the thawing of permafrost and changing the oceans. For cities it concludes that some aspects of these changes may be amplified including heat, flooding and sea level rise. It emphasises that global averages mean extremes at various times and locations.

In general it concludes that carbon dioxide ($CO_2$) emissions are the main drivers of climate change. Decarbonisation remains the global priority to mitigate dangerous climate change.

## The world post COVID 19

Responses to the COVID 19 pandemic have accelerated social and economic changes that are now seen as having been inevitable. These include working from home, home education and Internet shopping and deliveries, which all have accentuated the need for housing that can meet these needs. They have also highlighted the need for effective public health, welfare and education services that can meet public needs, regardless of relative affluence and prosperity. Nevertheless, economic and social disparities have been accentuated with areas of multiple-deprivation suffering
most.

**It can be concluded energy efficient and flexible low cost housing remains a priority both for the renewal and regeneration of the existing stock and new building. A universal basic income, or Citizen's Dividend, discussed later, becomes a factor in addressing unacceptable social and economic disparities.**

## Globalisation and automation

Mass employment in manufacturing and services has been, and is being, automated rapidly. Artificial Intelligence (AI) is doing to thinking skills what robotics has done to manual skills.

The global implication would seem to be that manufacturing that was out sourced to low labour cost countries may well relocate nearer to markets and that service employment, in offices or at home, may significantly diminish, with consequences for commuting and city centres.

Activities that require human thinking and emotional skills, such as research, caring and educating and those related to the specialities of local and regional economies may take on greater significance in the future. The pattern of work may be "portfolio" employment in a number of occupations in the market, in self-employment or volunteering, supported by a universal basic income.

**This is the strategic employment context in prospect.**

## The financialisation of everything

Financialisation has meant putting a price on everything that does not always reflect its real value to society. Such as caring services. As market employment is increasingly affected by automation it might be expected that services requiring human qualities will be re-valued.

**They may become a primary component of the portfolio economy.**

# Global warming and environmental impact - Migration and biodiversity

## Mitigation - Stabilising climate change

Climate change, or more precisely global warming, has been recognised for some three decades, by the United Nations, to be the most serious threat facing humanity. Only as more has become known about the rate of warming and its widespread and catastrophic consequences has the need for urgent action become globally apparent and accepted. At last the range of action that is now urgently required, to mitigate these consequences and stabilise warming at a level that will enable human life on earth to be sustained, has become clear through the work of the UN Framework Convention on Climate Change, the UNFCCC.

The current position is set out in the Paris Agreement of 2015. *"The Paris Agreement central aim is to strengthen the global response to the threat of climate change by keeping a global temperature rise this century well below 2 degrees Celsius above pre-industrial levels and to pursue efforts to limit the temperature increase even further to 1.5 degrees Celsius"*.

# Levelling Up - Good Governance and Effective Planning

The European Union (EU) seeks a 55% reduction in greenhouse gas emissions by 2030, which includes the following specific targets to help meet the needs of the Paris Agreement.

- 40% cuts in greenhouse gas emissions (from 1990 levels)
- 32% share for renewable energy
- 32.5% improvement in energy efficiency

The EU aims to be "climate neutral" by 2050 with an economy with net zero greenhouse gas emissions.

As Europe's 272 metropolitan regions (see Appendix 2) contain some 70%, or about 300 million, of the continent's 448 million population (Eurostat 2020), it is not unreasonable to assume that they should assume responsibility for

achieving this percentage of EU targets for 2030 and its aim for 2050. In reality, the objective should be to decarbonise as fast and completely as possible. Decarbonisation is taken to include all dangerous greenhouse gases, reduced to their carbon dioxide equivalents.

## Levelling Up - Good Governance and Effective Planning

The challenge for strategic planning is to clarify the most effective measures that can be taken to promote decarbonisation both by reducing emissions and increasing the production of renewable energy. Europe's urban areas are the major source of carbon energy consumption and consequent greenhouse gas emissions and the reduction of demand, through energy saving, and a transfer of supply to urban renewable energy, are the most effective actions that can be taken. This is why the European Union has set the targets it has for these priorities.

The term global warming gives the impression of a rising curve that can be slowed and reversed over time. There are other scenarios, which foresee "tipping points" that lead to irreversible and catastrophic change. For example, from the melting of the Antarctic polar ice cap and the loss of Arctic sea ice. This could arise from the warming of the sea and lead to global sea rises of metres. Such sea rise could be compounded by river floodwater that cannot discharge. Many of Europe's major metropolitan areas are on the coast, on deltas or river estuaries and will become more vulnerable to flooding.

Climate change will fundamentally affect the "carrying capacity" of the globe and its ability to support life and biodiversity. In the context of a global population that is forecast by the United Nations (UN) to grow from 7 billion in 2011 to 9.7 billion in 2050 there is likely to be increased migration north from equatorial regions experiencing desertification and from southern regions facing drought and very high temperatures. External and internal migration will become an increasing issue for urban Europe.

Such potentially dramatic physical, environmental and socio-economic change compounds the need for urgent action to mitigate further global warming and adapt to the change that is now inevitable.

The Climate Change Advisory Group (CCAG) has reported that global warming has already reached 1.25 degrees Celsius and that on the basis of current global decarbonisation pledges it will exceed 3 degrees Celsius. On this basis it concludes that not only is the reduction of greenhouse gas emissions necessary but also measures to remove carbon dioxide from the atmosphere and repair the global damage already caused and in prospect. This is the technological, social and economic challenge for the future.

## Urban energy saving and renewable energy generation

There are two routes to energy saving. Firstly, to reduce energy using activities and, secondly, to use energy more efficiently. This means reducing waste.

Within urban areas the primary activities are within the building stock and on the transportation network. Higher density development that is well integrated with public transport is more energy efficient. Low-density development and urban sprawl is less energy efficient and mitigates against walking, cycling and the use of public transport as energy efficient modes of transport. So urban form, of itself, can enable or diminish the energy efficient use of land and buildings. Strategic planning has a role to play in sustaining energy efficient compact, or polycentric, metropolitan regions.

Europe's building stock is now either old or historic or newer but built during the era of a plentiful supply of low cost carbon energy (coal, oil and gas) when the implications of greenhouse gas emissions were unrecognised. Energy wastage was less of an issue either environmentally or financially. There are, therefore, two steps to be taken to reduce waste. Firstly, with older and historic buildings the scope to insulate interiors and exteriors of heritage significance may be constrained. But thin film technologies, for insulation and heating, are available that are less intrusive. Secondly, the newer building stock can be remodelled and insulated and all stock can benefit from roof, floor and window insulation. These are the most important steps that can be taken within metropolitan regions to contribute to their energy neutrality as early as possible.

Less obvious is the potential for the urban fabric of metropolitan Europe to become a major source of renewable energy generation and the possibility of metropolitan regions becoming largely self sufficient in renewable energy. There are the well-established technologies for domestic solar roof panels and the equivalent of small "solar farms" on extensive low-rise factories or retail centres. But beyond this are the emerging thin film

technologies that enable high-rise buildings to capture solar energy from their wall surfaces. Solar energy is currently the cheapest available.

These sources of solar renewable energy may be supplemented by local wind turbines but these will not be as significant in their potential. In all cases excess renewable energy generation can be used to produce hydrogen, as a means of energy storage and as a source of energy itself. The hydrogen economy is discussed later.

## Urban mobility - Commuting and the need to travel

The decarbonisation of public transport networks, through the introduction of electrified light tram or heavy rail systems, and their integration with electric or hydrogen fuelled feeder bus services, will complement the strategic action taken to make the building stock energy neutral.

But reducing the need to travel and, in particular, commuting from suburbs to city centres, will also reduce energy use. Congestion charges in city centres have been found to reduce discretionary non-essential car travel and working from home reduces commuting (see the world post COVID that follows).

Car ownership has become less attractive as car usage is discouraged through parking and congestion charges. On street parking is an environmental problem functionally and visually in congested urban areas. What is actually required is urban mobility and mobility on demand, through emerging technologies such as driverless vehicles, may be where the future lies in metropolitan regions. There would then be far fewer vehicles and feeder bus services would find it easier and more efficient to operate. Walking and cycling would become safer and more attractive.

## The hydrogen economy - Feedstock, storage and source of power

The hydrogen economy is the natural partner to a renewable energy future that is founded on solar and wind. These are intermittent energy sources and a means of storing off peak electricity production for peak electricity use is required. The production and storage of hydrogen is the answer by using electricity to separate hydrogen and oxygen from water by electrolysis.

Hydrogen can then be used as an alternative to natural gas or converted back to electricity on demand. Hydrogen can also be used in heavy vehicles, buses and trains as an alternative to electricity and batteries. It can help create alternatives to aviation fuels, using carbon dioxide from carbon capture and storage (CCS), which are the most difficult to replace. A win-win.

There is an argument for making substantial overprovision of wind and solar power in order to be able to provide a regulated renewable energy supply, through a transcontinental European grid, and to produce hydrogen as a fuel and a feedstock. Such a strategy could also be adopted regionally to provide a secure and sustainable energy future on which to build a competitive economy.

## Transportation - Goods and tourism - Aviation and Shipping

Globalisation has resulted in huge flows of energy, manufactured goods, raw materials, food and produce (animal feed) around the world. Renewable energy, automation and robotics and climate change will have a material effect on these. It seems probable that cheap labour markets will be of less attraction and that food production for domestic consumption, rather than export, will predominate as scarcity grows. Shipping flows of low value goods may decline with high value trade, by ship or airfreight, continuing.

Large container ships and cruise ships, using low-grade diesel fuel, are currently a highly polluting form of transport and a major source of green house gas emissions. A transfer to hydrogen power is an obvious solution.

37

Tourism is the worlds largest industry. In recent decades it has been founded on cheap flights that do not pay their real cost in terms of greenhouse gas emissions. Emissions at high altitude have a disproportionately high greenhouse gas effect and aviation will be one of the most difficult issues to be tackled if global warming is to be held at, or reduced to, the levels required by the UNFCCC. Aviation fuels have the high-energy output required for take off and viable alternatives are not yet in prospect, although hydrogen may yet provide one. Electric and hybrid planes can use battery power for ground manoeuvres and have been developed for short haul flights.

EU transport policy is to favour high-speed trains (HST) over short haul internal flights under 400 kilometres. These comprise the majority of flights, for tourism purposes. Their taxation does not offset their impact. There are many activities that use offsetting, usually through forestry planting, to enable them to continue functioning in the short term. However, it is clear that forestation is needed on a global scale, of itself, to absorb carbon dioxide and the more it is used to offset emission increases the less it can be used to reduce them. Offsetting is not sustainable.

As well as a shift from short-haul aviation to HST the EU is also seeking a shift from road freight to short sea shipping (SSS). The target is a shift of 30% of road freight, over 300 kilometres, to other modes by 2030. It is currently estimated that 30% of all freight movements within Europe are carried by sea, primarily by SSS. The major interchange ports of Europe will have a key role to play in facilitating a further modal shift to SSS and connection to a European rail freight network.

Metropolitan regions that have major ports, transhipment hubs, and hub airports in their areas will be faced with their emission impacts and be dependent on global changes in shipping and aviation energy use to enable them to decarbonise. They will be able to decarbonise port and airport land functions, transferring to renewable energy and hydrogen, but will be dependent on global and EU regulations to progress the decarbonisation of ships and planes, as they are doing for road vehicles and trains.

## Transportation - Road and rail

There are two strategic aspects of road transport that arise in metropolitan regions. Firstly, the greenhouse gas emissions of diesel and petrol engines and, secondly, the congestion that arises in urban areas from vehicular use.

Vehicle manufacturers are now on a clear path to decarbonisation through the interim introduction of hybrid (electric/carbon fuels) vehicles and, by 2030 or so, through a move to electric and hydrogen vehicles. As this transition proceeds it can be expected that battery and charging technologies will develop, for example, through induction charging in roads.

As vehicles, especially cars, spend much of their life unused there is scope for electric vehicle battery capacity, linked to the grid, to be used as national back up. With heavy vehicles, such as buses and trucks, there is also the option of hydrogen being used, through fuel cells, to replace carbon fuels.

It can be concluded that the issue of vehicular greenhouse gas emissions can be resolved through widespread electrification. The environmental impact of vehicle and battery manufacture can be addressed through their longer life and eventual recycling.

However, there remains the key issue of vehicle use and the extent to which this reflects the real need for mobility or is discretionary. It is clear from congestion charging that much vehicular use is not essential and that vehicle ownership, in high density metropolitan urban areas, involves high costs (tax, insurance, fuel, parking and congestion). The real issue is the need for urban mobility.

The strategic public transport network, when well connected within urban areas by local feeder services, walking and cycling networks, can provided good accessibility to and from centres for commuting, comparison goods shopping, higher education and leisure. However, commuting and retailing are being affected by working from home and Internet shopping and home delivery. As long as centres are sustained for multi-purpose and specialised trips then the public transport system, strategic and local, will have a continuing and strong role to play.

For local trips within urban areas there is the prospect of driverless electric vehicles being able to provide mobility on demand without the multiple costs of car ownership. Congestion on roads and through on street parking could be reduced with significant emission reduction and local environmental benefits.

## Sustainable food supplies

It is clear that, as with energy, waste is a major factor in greenhouse gas emissions from food production and consumption. However, food waste can be recycled and reused as a fertiliser to offset these. The key issue for sustainability is where and how food is produced and its environmental impact. The issue of "food miles" arises when the impact of its

transportation is comparable to the impact of its production. Clearly, the basic approach of eat locally and seasonally applies. Intensive farming, of arable crops and livestock, has resulted in cheap and plentiful food at some environmental cost. Non-seasonal food imports, from across the globe, can also have such costs. Food retailers are now paying great attention to ethical production and the climate change impact of chains of supply.

For Europe's metropolitan regions, facing the prospect of climate change affecting both the quantity of imported food available and its environmental cost, it seems wise to maximise regional and local self-sufficiency in food and to only export specialised products or surpluses. The rediscovery of regional and local food products can form the basis of a local food economy and culture, with all its quality of life and climate change benefits.

There has been huge growth in the eating of meat worldwide. Animals that produce methane as part of their digestive process are a significant source of greenhouse gas emissions. There appears no alternative to the recognition that meat eating needs to become a selective and limited part of European diets.

# The world post COVID 19 – How the need for change became obvious

## Governance and COVID 19

Town planning has its origins in the responses that emerged from the epidemics of the past including, for example, cholera and recognition of the need for light and air, an end to over crowding and very high urban population densities, clean water and effective waste disposal.

The COVID 19 global pandemic has revealed some truths about effective governance. Co-ordinated action was found to be necessary at the national, regional, metropolitan and local levels in order to achieve the common objective of containing or eliminating the virus. All levels of governance needed to share these objectives and to support the means of achieving them. Public support and compliance was crucial to success. The public interest was clearly recognised.

Isolation emerged as a key means of containing the virus and it became clear that the level at which this needed to be enforced was the region or metropolitan region. These are the levels at which social and economic inter action plays out and needs to be controlled. In some European countries a tiered approach to containment was adopted with different measures applying in different regions. The important point for governance is that the social and economic interaction at the regional level was recognised. As a result it became the level for effective pandemic planning.

## Austerity and financial resources

The 2008 financial crash, where financial institutions devised products to spread and minimise risk that in reality turned out to compound risk, resulted in their "bail out" with public funds, which then had to be repaid with a period of cut back in public expenditure and austerity. Economic growth was diminished, public services constrained and poverty and disadvantage increased. Basic human needs grew but were unmet, for example, for affordable housing. This was the experience in many European countries including the poorest.

This policy stands in contrast to the European response to the COVID 19 pandemic and its financial consequences. Public expenditure to support employment has been provided on a massive scale, at a level equal to post war reconstruction in Europe. Various ways of funding this have been explored including perpetual government bonds that only pay interest and do not involve capital repayment.

The financial problem is that a second period of austerity would further damage an already COVID 19 damaged European economy. What has also emerged is that government funding can be devised to meet national priorities, in a crisis, and that longer term borrowing at low interest rates can be wise. The real issue for the future is what national expenditure priorities now are? These are discussed in this chapter.

## Pandemic management - Lessons for regional planning

A lesson for governance from the experience of the COVID 19 pandemic is that an effective regional or metropolitan region level is a necessity for coordinated action by health, welfare, employment, transport, housing, educational and security services. All have a role to play in implementing a strategy of containment or elimination. All have a similar role to play in implementing a regional strategy for economic growth or recovery and renewal in more normal times.

The pandemic has required social controls to keep levels of infection and care at levels that a health service can cope with whilst maintaining other necessary services. It has revealed any shortcomings that there may be in care for the vulnerable and any needs that there may be for better housing. Above all it has required a high level of support for those whose livelihoods, whether from employment or self-employment, have been curtailed or lost.

All of these needs may have existed to a greater or lesser degree before the pandemic but have been highlighted by it. The lesson from the pandemic is that a regional dimension exists to most social and economic crises or periods of rapid change, requiring effective governance to manage the response that the public interest requires. Deprivation and disparities

Levels of infection by COVID 19 have been found to be highest in areas of multiple social, economic and environmental deprivation. Indicators of deprivation can include unemployment, welfare support, educational achievement, poor housing conditions and overcrowding. In such circumstances it becomes difficult, if not impossible, to meet the requirements of pandemic isolation such as working from home or home education. Any social disparities that exist within a region have been exacerbated.

The pandemic has revealed where the social and economic needs of a region are most acute. They are frequently compounded by environmental shortcomings that limit opportunities for recreation and some relief from isolation. The needs of such areas of multiple-deprivation need to be identified and addressed at the metropolitan region level if they are to be given the priority they require.

## Health inequalities

Multiple-deprivation frequently means poverty, poor diet and poor housing. Health is prejudiced as a consequence, leaving people vulnerable. COVID 19 has exposed such vulnerabilities and inequalities.

Health provision across Europe may involve the public and private sectors and will require the allocation of resources on the basis of need. This is easiest when a strong public health service exists. It means the provision of a network of general practitioner local health services, possibly through health centres, and regional hospitals providing specialist consultant services and care.

Health and welfare services are closely inter-related, especially in care for the elderly. Care for the elderly is a cultural as well as a health and welfare issue. For example, it may be at home, in "sheltered housing" with care support, in care homes or in hospital.

Planning for an integrated health and welfare service, for all ages and social and economic circumstances and levels of need, requires strategic planning at the metropolitan region level. It will evolve with changing demographic and household needs that can be most effectively foreseen, and provided for, at the regional level.

## Housing inequalities

Housing provision across Europe is made by the public and private sectors, for rental or ownership. Nations have different attitudes to rental and ownership arising from different perceptions of security, freedom of action and cost. In some countries there is a long established tradition of private rental, with secure tenancies and controlled rents. In others there is an equally strong tradition of home ownership, with freedom to move by selling and freedom to make modifications to meet personal or family needs. In assessing future housing needs and prospective demand, planning will have regard to the likely tenure choices in a region.

Housing need is a consequence of population change, household formation, housing standards and provision. Housing demand is a function of the housing market and affordability. The public sector fulfils the function of rental housing provider of last resort to ensure that homelessness does not arise and that all have affordable access to a decent standard of housing. The private sector, to rent or to buy, seeks a return on its investment and affordability is only an issue in keeping the private housing stock marketable.

The balance between housing need and demand varies across Europe but social disparities can be widened if there is not a mix of tenure opportunities within a community and single tenures prevail over large housing areas. COVID 19 has demonstrated the importance of housing when working from home, home educating and participating in life long learning. These trends are likely to be sustained and, taken with the issue of multi generational housing, will affect both need and demand. Inequality arises when only the private sector can respond to such changes.

The housing market, for home ownership, has been distorted by property becoming an attractive investment in times of low interest rates. Housing inequality has been compounded by the difference between those financially able to join the "housing ladder" and those who cannot. This is a function of credit rating and the ability to borrow.

## Employment and income inequalities

Employment has become increasingly insecure as support services are out sourced by large employers and automation reduces both manufacturing and service employment. Self-employment has increased. The unemployment support offered by the state varies across Europe but often comprises benefits that are income and circumstance dependent.

Across Europe the COVID 19 pandemic has closed places of work or led to working from home where housing makes this possible. Suddenly employees at all levels found themselves dependent on the state. The importance of a basic living wage became obvious and housing conditions that enabled home working became much more important. It seems that this shift may become permanent in many cases.

It would seem that countries with lower disparities between incomes are more cohesive and more able to take collective action when this is required.

## Education inequalities

Early pre school education enables primary school children to make a confident start. Thereafter, mixed economies depend on high quality public sector schools to enable their pupils to take advantage of the opportunities offered by higher education. Good housing plays an important role in good education, especially when education from home is required or on offer. This becomes even more so in enabling all to take advantage of on line higher education or life long learning.

## Health services and caring

Once a major health emergency arises the importance of subsidiarity in governance quickly becomes apparent. Countries with strong regional, metropolitan and local levels of governance are able to devise and implement effective strategies and to provide the integrated health and caring services that are required. Strategic planning and social services are able to contribute by identifying areas of multiple-deprivation, or poor housing conditions where there is the greatest need for health and care services.

## Working from home - Internet shopping

The Internet has enabled major changes to be made in how work is carried out and how shopping needs are met, on line, from home. This focus on the home, which may be an enduring change, places even more emphasis on the need for good quality housing that meets the need for family and personal space. In multi generational homes this is even more so.

## Subsidiarity becomes operational - Integrated national, regional and local action

The COVID 19 pandemic forced into being the recognition of regions and metropolitan regions as the key levels at which strategies involving a range of control measures could be applied to differing circumstances. They demonstrated the value of an integrated approach, based on the concept of subsidiarity, to a strategic issue, the pandemic. The implications for the future of good governance are clear. The same principles should be applied when other strategic issues, such as multiple-deprivation, are being addressed.

## Some conclusions

The experience of the COVID 19 pandemic has shown, in a mixed economy, firstly, the value of well resourced and planned public services, particularly health, welfare and education. And in resilience, as a planning factor, to be built in to them.

Secondly, the value of good housing to enable households to use the home for multi generational activities, particularly work and education but also socialising. And the need for space and flexibility in housing. The social and economic consequences of poor housing conditions and overcrowding have been exposed.

Thirdly, that areas of multiple deprivation in metropolitan regions are a result of widening social and economic disparities and, in a pandemic, of vulnerability. The vulnerability of all those in social and economic need, and particularly the aged, has become an issue for action.

All of these issues will need a strategic planning response in the future.

# Globalisation and automation - The future of work

## Globalisation - Labour costs and transportation

The past fifty years has seen a seismic shift in the way goods and services are produced and distributed. A truly global economy has emerged in which all countries now participate to a greater or lesser extent. It has seen the rise of great disparities between rich and poor countries to the extent that the most affluent in the world, the G20* countries, now generate about 80%** of global wealth (by Gross Domestic Product - GDP). Trade flows around the globe have increased many-fold with shipping now carrying around 90% of world trade***.

There are huge implications for global warming and climate change with the consumption patterns of wealthy countries generating, directly and indirectly, most of the greenhouse gases. It is within the G20 that the necessary mitigation action is required most.

The production of consumer goods has passed, primarily, from richer countries to those with lower labour costs. However, as automation progresses, and high levels of consumption by richer countries become increasingly unsustainable, it might be expected that production will move closer to markets. Even with the prospective switch from diesel-electric power to hydrogen-electric power for shipping, transportation costs, including their environmental costs, may still make production closer to markets more economic and sustainable.

In these circumstances globalisation may change in nature from, primarily, producer and consumer relationships to mutual trade in raw materials, finished goods and food, where there are tradable surpluses or specialities. Most importantly, trade in carbon fuels such as oil and gas can be expected to diminish as renewable energy takes over.

* Argentina, Australia, Brazil, Canada, China, France, Germany, India, Indonesia, Italy, Japan, Republic of Korea, Mexico, Russia, Saudi Arabia, South Africa, Turkey, United Kingdom, United States, and the European Union.

** German Federal Statistics Office

*** UNCTAD

# Automation and its impact on manufacturing and services

Automation has had a huge impact on manufacturing jobs and is having a comparable effect on service jobs. This would not necessarily mean that such jobs are lost in their entirety but that significant aspects of them would be replaced. If thinking can be replaced by an algorithm it will be. For example, much stock market trading is now done on this basis as is banking and insurance. The assessment of risk had become automated and a common on-line function.

It seems probable that jobs with a high need for human qualities, such as empathy and caring, will be needed more as will those needing higher levels of thinking. Mass employment in manufacturing and services seems likely to have been lost on a permanent basis, with implications for job security, pensions and taxation.

Such a prospective change in the pattern of employment has implications for town and city centres, the support services they provide, commuting and public transport. If a degree of working from home becomes a permanent aspect of life, resulting from the response to the COVID 19 pandemic, then these changes are likely to be compounded. They will then have significant implications for strategic planning.

## The Portfolio economy - Employment and occupations

It is possible to foresee a continuing rise in self-employment, something that has already happened from the out-sourcing of services from companies and businesses. Short-term contracts with little security are now commonplace. Families and individuals are having to respond by seeking a range, or "portfolio", of remunerative opportunities. There is no shortage of basic human needs that require to be met either through employment in the public or private sectors. The issue is the extent to which these will be funded and can be afforded. Such needs can also be met through occupations in the voluntary sectors.

## A Citizens Dividend - universal basic income

This uncertain future for full time employment paying good salaries with security, holidays, sick pay and pensions raises the important issue of a universal basic income, provided by the state, to underpin the prospective portfolio employment future. At present, state benefits are often targeted at, or to, certain groups or categories of need. In rapidly changing economic times this approach can lead to delayed responses and personal hardships. This is the fundamental case for a universal basic income.

There is an argument, advocated by David Susskind in his book "A World Without Work", to call this a Citizens Dividend, on the argument that all, over their lifetimes, contributed to the stability, security and well-being of the state and all should be able to benefit from, and have a return from, this "social capital". Such a dividend might be pitched at a level to meet basic human needs in a mixed economy and would depend on the extent to which these are met by the state and/or the market in whole or in part.

It would remove much of the anxiety in society about future livelihoods and enable individuals, families and society in general to plan for the future with more certainty and confidence. It would be a measure supporting social cohesion and the limitation of disparities. It would help to address pressing issues such as poverty and homelessness that have arisen in even the most prosperous of European societies.

## Taxation and public expenditure

A consequence of the changing prospects for secure employment is the level of tax that might be raised in the future from income tax. This may need to be compensated for by environmental taxes designed to help reach EU decarbonisation goals. Many aspects of economic life do not presently pay their full environmental costs, including energy generation using carbon fuels, urban development, consumer goods production and transportation.

There is a debate, which all European countries and regions need to have with their electorates, about future sources and levels of taxation to provide public services meeting basic human needs in a mixed economy.

## Pensions

It is said that an indication of a civilised society is how it treats and cares for the elderly. Some economies can be harsh in their attitudes to aging with an unspoken view that the economically less active are less valuable to society. This is reflected in the level of state pension provision that is made. Anxieties about aging can be alleviated by a Citizens Dividend that lasts into later life.

## Self-sufficiency and sustainability

It would seem to be wise, in the global economy that is emerging, for regions and metropolitan regions to make provision for the highest level of self-sufficiency that they are able to achieve in meeting the basic human needs of energy, food and water supplies on a sustainable basis. The export of regional surpluses or specialities would then provide an additional strength to the regional economy. Such an approach has implications for the strategic planning of a region and its future.

## Regional and local economies

As globalisation changes what is traded, and between whom, it might be expected that there will be a rise in the significance of regional and local economies. They can look to import substitution and self sufficiency to start with and to their particular regional and local resources to enable them to develop a diverse and sustainable economy. They can then export their surpluses, which may be substantial, and specialities, which may include University and other research institutions knowledge and innovation and their tradable outcomes.

At the local level there will be scope to meet the need for personal and household services through exchange and the equivalent of a local "e-bay" for services rather than goods. There is no limit to the occupations that could be made available on a voluntary, exchange or paid basis. In the portfolio economy occupations could involve participating in the unpaid and paid economy, given the underlying financial support of a Citizens Dividend.

## e-commerce, e-education and e-health and welfare

*Urban densification very much depends on smart technologies that allow and require smart management of urban complexity. - Klaus R. Kunzmann.*

The COVD-19 pandemic that has resulted in the "lockdown" of whole countries, where people are confined to their homes for long periods and only allowed out to shop, has given rise to e-commerce of all kinds including not only retailing but also personal and corporate business services. On line transactions now dominate in many sectors. The consequence has been a rise in logistics, warehousing and distribution, as a key function in metropolitan regions.

This has also translated to education, health and welfare where public services have also had to go on line in order to continue to meet their obligations. Where retailers have been able to draw on their automated warehouses and large stores as distribution bases, the public sector has had to draw on its infrastructure of schools, hospitals and governance offices. They have become the distribution hubs for knowledge, advice and supplies.

For economies that have privatised and outsourced there has been a recognition that good governance requires a maintained core capability to provide its key services in the areas of education, health and welfare. The care of the young, the vulnerable and older citizens has been seen to be, as it always has been, a function of good governance in the public interest.

Perhaps e-health may have the greatest implication for health planning. The function of hospitals, and their related local health services, may change to become specialist centres for treatment with diagnosis, prescription and care becoming more localised and home based.

Higher education and life–long learning is already well established and available as an e-education service. What COVID 19 has done is to introduce such services at the primary and secondary education levels.

There are strategic implications for such changes, foremost of which is the provision of reliable high-speed domestic Internet connections but of comparable significance is the need for greater space in housing so that it can fulfil its function as a base for e-education and e-health and welfare as well as the e-commerce that the consumer society is now so familiar with.

As well as the adaptation of existing housing and the modification of the new, there will also be a need within communities to provide somewhere, such as libraries or purpose built e-hubs, for the provision of e-services of all kinds to those without access to on line services. In effect, a development of the e-cafes that already serve social society.

The COVID 19 pandemic, and its financial and taxation consequences, is having the effect of accelerating the consideration of numerous ways in which public services can be provided within the overall concept of "smart cities". These use electronic big data to manage their resources and operations more efficiently.

The electronic dimension to regional and metropolitan strategic planning has become clear, through the responses needed to the COVID 19 pandemic.

## Artificial Intelligence (AI)

Manual work has been automated to the extent that only the more skilled and specialised activities remain. Such automation has advanced with the computerisation of supply, manufacturing and distribution. The value of logistics and the automation of food supply, distribution and sale by supermarket chains was dramatically illustrated during the COVID 19 pandemic.

But AI, through the acquisition and analysis of data on a very large scale (big data), is now able to go beyond robotics and logistics. It can make decisions that were previously the preserve of human intelligence in the areas of assessment, diagnosis and prescription, for example, in the fields of medicine, education, finance and urban systems management.

There has always been a debate about the value of automation of manual and mental human activities in liberating humanity from the less rewarding economic activities at the price of a quantitative loss of

65

employment. The argument is that such change then creates more opportunities for higher quality and more rewarding human activities such as research, caring and teaching. This should be a purpose of AI but it will require promoted and supported social and economic change to facilitate it.

# The financialisation of everything - Development as an asset

## Financialisation

There is an underlying problem with market economies that put a price on everything, all goods and all services, based on demand, or on created demand, and supply and, in the process, under value human services to meet basic human needs. The COVID 19 pandemic has shown that even advanced economies cannot survive without "front line" workers to keep basic public services operating. In a portfolio economy such work needs to be re-evaluated and re-valued in financial terms.

## Consumption and global warming

High levels of consumption for the developed world means benefitting from the low production costs of labour forces in the developing world. Major retailers in the developed world are now finding that they need to become more aware of the true social and environmental costs of these trading practices and to be conscious of supply trains and their ethical acceptability.

If there is one thing that the developed world, the G20, could do to support the mitigation of greenhouse gas emissions it would be to lower its levels of consumption, both personal and corporate, and to fully embrace the idea of the "Circular Economy", which aims to reuse and recycle as much as is possible and to avoid waste. As with energy, consumer waste is a major source of avoidable greenhouse gas emissions. The clothing industry has a major part to play in all of this by producing longer lasting products and redirecting fashion to the sustainable rather than the cheap and disposable.

## Interest rates, investment and asset values

In a world in which secure investments with a return are hard to find, and interest rates are low, there has been a global move to investment in assets, foremost of which are properties. Such investments have led to property, sometimes increasing in value faster than incomes, being left unused simply to give a return or avoid a loss and taking housing beyond general affordability. Governments have had to intervene in property markets that may be international in character to ensure national and regional affordability. For example, by providing subsidies on property or to prospective owners or tenants.

An alternative to this is for the public sector to make the necessary affordable provision for regional or local economic or housing needs, for example, start up business premises or affordable housing. This was the practice by UK New Town Development Corporations where subsidised promotional business and factory premises were associated with low cost rental housing for incoming and key workers. In this case the intention was to create value and promote growth. In metropolitan regions the same measures could be used to meet regional and local needs and opportunities where property has become a financial rather than a productive or necessary investment. The UK has used urban Development Corporations for this very purpose.

## Development pressures and speculation

The value of land as the resource through which development as an asset can be realised makes it vulnerable to speculative pressures. Land banks are built up in the expectation that sites will eventually be released. Development is then, primarily, the means of realising the increased value of the land. This process puts pressure on any planning system to accept development proposals that do not accord with an agreed regional development strategy and local plans. Essentially, the increased value of land arises from the region and community in which it lies and attempts have been made to capture

69

this, in whole or in part, for the community. Community land taxes have been adopted and these will become relevant again as sources of income tax, through employment, decline.

## Housing and inflation - Ownership as an asset

There have been circumstances when inflation has been running at high levels and, in effect, paying off mortgages. This has left a generation of homeowners with valuable assets created by external circumstances and now being passed on within families. It is in contrast to those renting, who have not participated in property inflation, and those now seeking to buy who find home ownership beyond them. This is particularly so for the young and those working in now expensive metropolitan housing markets.

In these circumstances housing need can become critical but unmet. One response is to subsidise building costs, through grants and loans, and buyer costs through low deposit, low cost mortgages based on multiple incomes over extended periods. These were the very practices that led to the financial crisis of 2012 when negative equity became a major, but unquantifiable, issue.

The more straightforward response to housing need is to build energy efficient public sector housing for rent at scale. Such a programme can focus on Brownfield sites and support wider strategies of urban renewal and regeneration. Rising housing values have enabled the conversion of redundant industrial and commercial buildings, many of heritage value, into apartments. Such changes may now be harnessed to revitalise city and town centres where retailing has been adversely affected by on-line Internet sales.

## Housing affordability - The need for a rental sector

Home ownership involves more than being able to afford a mortgage. Housing requires on-going maintenance and modernisation involving income and capital expenditure. There are sections of society, young and old, for whom ownership will be impractical and unsuitable. Once home ownership reaches beyond about 70% of households it may become unaffordable in income and capital terms, for example, to those on pensions or low incomes. There will always, therefore, need to be a significant rental-housing sector, whether public or private.

Good affordable housing is the base from which participation in all social and economic activities flows. Without secure and affordable housing it is impossible, in todays Europe, to fully participate in and contribute to the "Communitaire" society. Family life is impossible without it. Social cohesion is diminished without it. An address is the first requirement for most employment and welfare support.

Planning for housing is, therefore, one of the most important functions of good governance at the regional and local levels. It must establish need and how to meet it, in terms of quantity, quality and affordability. It will assess the existing stock and the need for renewal and the related need for new build programmes on Brownfield and/or Greenfield locations. It will ensure that locations are developable, dealing with any underlying constraints such as ground pollution or stability, and bring these forward on a rolling basis.

## Capital and disparities

The financialisation and privatisation of services and resources that were once regarded as communitaire and part of the common good, such as housing, health, education and caring and water, energy and transportation, has contributed to wide, and growing, disparities between those with assets and those without. Between those living with and from wealth and those living from labour.

## Levelling Up - Good Governance and Effective Planning

A number of commentators, mentioned in the Acknowledgements, see a Wealth Tax, coordinated on a global scale, as part of the policy response. They also see reform of the banking system to include public sector banking administering National and Regional Investment Banks and citizens retail banks as a financial framework within which to give citizens the opportunity to take a stake in their economies and have access to financial services more related to their needs. To have access to regional, local and personal financial services on a not for profit basis.

It appears that the developed economies are unlikely to now be able to achieve and sustain the high economic growth rates that would allow disparities to be reduced, over time, through economic policy. If a future lies with regional and local economies based on increased self-sufficiency, sustainability, natural resources, surpluses and specialisation then it would seem that present financial institutions orientated to the management of assets and wealth will not be what is needed. Financial services will be required that better serve the needs of the economies within which they lie.

# What needs planning – The really important issues

## Housing need - The relationships between housing market areas, migration, household formation and tenure

The starting point for the definition and quantification of housing need is housing market areas. These are the broad localities, within a metropolitan region, within which households search to meet their housing needs. They can be local needs, for example, from changing household size, or regional needs, for example, from those coming into a region for employment. Their search areas, in either case, will emerge from house sales records (where selling and where buying) and rental records, if in the public sector.

Demographic forecasts and prospective household formation rates enable the planning process to assess the probability of emerging need in housing market areas. Assumptions can be made about tenure choice (ownership or rental) and the fitness of the existing housing stock to meet future needs. There may be issues of housing stock quality and "fit" (to house the households foreseen). Paradoxically, housing need can continue to grow even with population decline, if household size becomes smaller through aging or single parenthood.

A key issue in assessing housing need will be migration. Migration from a region may take place if the regional economy is in decline or to a region if its economy is growing. So economic prospects are a factor in assessing prospective housing need and, in uncertain times, may require to be the subject of regular strategic planning review.

Assumptions about future housing need then have to be related to the housing stock in housing market areas. If the objective is to sustain the housing attraction of metropolitan areas then the fitness of the stock, in terms of dwelling sizes and quality, will be an issue. So a first consideration is the need for the renewal and regeneration of the existing stock. The next will be the capacity of vacant urban land and buildings to be recycled and reused sites, the Brownfield sites. They may require public expenditure to acquire them and make them developable. They may have a negative value because of their restoration costs. Brownfield sites offer the opportunity to promote mixed tenure housing areas and a housing mix that can remain more responsive to changing housing needs.

Only after this stage may the issue of the need to identify and release Greenfield sites arise. Even then the emphasis can be on supporting existing urban areas by choosing locations that are well related to public transport and support housing mix and choice in terms of dwelling types and tenure.

Housing need is dynamic and changing all the time as populations and households change. This becomes all the more apparent in times of structural economic change such as the present. The housing stock needs to reflect this by building in the flexibility to accommodate varying demands for working from home, home education, socialising, life long learning and multi-generational families.

The strategic planning process needs to reflect uncertainty by adopting a rolling process of need assessment and provision, perhaps on a two-year cycle to accommodate public consultation, political discussion and informed decision-making. Strategic planning needs to keep ahead of events if it is to fulfil its enabling role.

# Economic mobility and change - The new regional economies

The changing nature of globalisation and the future of work has been discussed earlier. In this context it was foreseen that regional economies could strengthen by placing more emphasis on their capability for self-sufficiency and sustainability. Their natural resources and specialist advantages can provide a focus for new regional economies. Such advantages, the so-called "unique selling points", or USP's, can provide the basis for their external economic relationships.

In the past there have been mass economic movements, from one country or region to another, from rural areas to cities and from areas of employment decline to areas of employment opportunity. These movements continue but the prospects would seem to be for less instability in the future as the opportunities for new mass employment decline through automation.

In these circumstances the role of strategic planning will be to recognise the need for the restructuring of the existing stock of commercial and industrial land and buildings, and its reuse and recycling, rather than to make provision for the release of a portfolio of major Greenfield sites with which to attract "mobile" and incoming industry. In the past such a portfolio was often felt to be a marketing necessity by regional development agencies. In practice it often ended up being used for other regional and local needs that might have been better located on renewed Brownfield sites.

## Centres matter - Changing roles and the future of retailing

A fundamental principle of metropolitan region strategies is that centres matter. They have always provided the focus for European social and economic life and have been able to adapt, through the ages, to value and retain their historic cores and reuse and recycle their building stock for new uses. A constant has been their ability to accommodate a wide range and variety of opportunities for socialising. Multi purpose trips are possible for shopping and leisure and a variety of employment is available. City and town centre living is particularly attractive to the young, to students and to the retired where accessibility to a range and variety of services is important.

Towns and cities grew up at points of accessibility, on rivers or coasts, and the accessibility of their centres remains a key attraction. Transportation networks within metropolitan regions are a key part of their infrastructure and fundamental to the continuing vitality and viability of their centres. To sustain centres on a continuing basis it will always be important to relate urban regeneration and renewal and urban extensions to the public transport network.

Retailing, from early markets, to covered arcades, to department stores and to malls has always been a core function of centres. Retailing could be considered as "comparison" shopping, for fashion or household "white goods", to "convenience" shopping, for food and essentials. A hierarchy of retailing from regional centres for high-end comparison shopping to local centres to meet convenience needs has emerged over time.

Out of centre retailing, in the form of malls, has been favoured at the expense of established centres where these were not felt capable of accommodating the emerging large retail units or increasing retail expenditure. Retail parks, comprising solely car-orientated warehouses, have emerged all over Europe and taken substantial retail expenditure from centres.

The irony now is that the viability of out of centre retailing, in the form of malls and retail parks, is now itself at risk from on-line Internet retailing. Once more the value of centres has emerged where

79

they can adapt to provide speciality services and goods that cannot be found in the retail chains that dominate Malls and Retail Parks. In effect, it has become a question of quality of experience where a vibrant street life and a variety of specialist shops and restaurants in an historic environment can be unique, attractive and competitive.

City and town centres have been found to need Managers to run them in the same way that Malls and Retail Parks are, giving attention to the quality of public spaces and their maintenance and the production of fun events and attractions. To capitalise on their unique selling points, their USP's.

## Mobility and transportation - Changing patterns of traffic generation

Perhaps the greatest change that is in prospect is an end to mass commuting within metropolitan regions. Travel to work to city and town centres will, of course, continue, with public transport the preferred option for energy saving, convenience and cost reasons. But the huge flows of office workers to city centres may diminish as working from home, established as a COVID 19 response, becomes a norm and routine office functions become more automated.

Most European metropolitan regions have radial rail public transport networks where cross-city journeys go through the centre. Peripheral road route routes enable journeys that by-pass a metropolitan area and journeys around the periphery by car or bus. It can be anticipated that a decentralisation of employment will mean more peripheral movements and fewer to the centre. Metropolitan areas may have to think in terms of circular public transport rail and bus routes.

If mobility on demand by driverless cars does become the future then this form of transport would be much more suited to peripheral and local movements than movements to the centre that result in continuing congestion.

## Safeguarding what we value - The built and natural environment

A core function of regional strategic planning is to define, recognise and safeguard natural and heritage resources of regional significance. Their significance might be because of their intrinsic value scientifically or historically, their relationships as component parts of regional networks, for example, of river valleys, or because of their value to communities for recreational or cultural purposes.

Safeguarding will mean protection, for example from prospective development and human pressures that would have an adverse impact on them, and can also mean interpretation to enable them to be accessed and used in an informed and sustainable way that does not prejudice their longer term viability.

The regional dimension to safeguarding the built and natural environment will be the valued locations themselves and, frequently, the networks of which they are part.

# The synoptic view – How the pieces fit together

## The synoptic view

Patrick Geddes (1854-1932), the Scottish biologist, sociologist, geographer and town planner, pioneered the concept of the "synoptic (all embracing) view" of regions. It asserts that regions are basic social, economic and environmental entities and that how they function needs to be considered in an integrated and holistic way. This thinking underlies the motivation for this book.

## A strategic vision - Where are we trying to get to?

Geddes used the Valley Section to illustrate the synoptic view. It was an illustration of a valley with the rural activities ranging from forestry and grazing on the slopes to arable farming on the valley floor and village street shops selling the produce from all levels of the valley. An integrated, sustainable, functional entity.

Strategic planners need this synoptic understanding of modern metropolitan regions and their much more complex social and economic relationships. From this understanding of the past and

83

present, and having regard to the wider national and international context at the time, they are well placed to explore the range of change that is likely in the future and the choices that are available to regional and local governance. To offer a strategic vision.

As the planning process proceeds, on a rolling basis, to update and review sectoral (housing, transportation etc.) and locational (centres, networks etc.) strategies, it will remain important to keep evaluating these against the overall strategic vision. To always keep in mind where the region is trying to get to.

## Foresight and what is probable or possible

Local authorities, regional and local, are invariably organised on a sectoral Departmental basis. Each may have statutory responsibilities and a requirement to consider future needs and how to meet them. They may be "predicting and providing" on the basis of their own forecasts. The transportation department may be surveying traffic flows, and origins and destinations, and making assumptions and predictions about future road and rail network capacity and development. Similarly, the education department may be making assumptions and predictions about pupil and student numbers and future school and college location and building.

84

Clearly, all departments will require to adopt common demographic, age group and household projections. Beyond these calculations a regional or local authority will also need to take a common view on the wider national and global context and on less predictable factors such as economic change and climate change. In effect, on the probable and the possible.

This is the substance of foresight and the capability to look to the future and its uncertainties and make an informed judgement about future problems and opportunities. All regional authorities would benefit from having a Foresight group or department with the corporate responsibility to provide an informed and synoptic view on medium and longer-term futures. In effect, scenarios and visions.

## Planning as an integrated rolling process

These would then provide an integrated context for sectoral strategies and programmes. Integration is vital to ensure, for example, that future land uses, that themselves generate movement and traffic, are integrated with the development of transportation networks. Perhaps most importantly the support services that are required to address the needs of areas of multiple deprivation, such as housing, welfare, education and health, need to be provided in an integrated way and with the environmental improvements that will also be necessary.

## Variable rates of change and the need for updates and review

Regional planning strategies need to be kept up to date if they are to fulfil their role in positively enabling development. But being up to date can vary with the issue concerned. For example, if change is rapid, or there are other uncertainties involved such as the availability of Brownfield land, then a short two year rolling process of review and updating may be necessary. Where strategies are safeguarding environmental resources for their longer-term leisure and recreational use then a five-year review may be more appropriate.

# Foresight – Taking the long view

## Directions, probabilities and possibilities

The prime purpose of foresight is to enable strategic policy directions to be taken with some insight into their implications. It allows preparations to be made for a range of possibilities. Strategic planning is all about the medium term 5-10/15 year period, where decisions remain to be taken, and beyond, to the longer term 15-25/30 year period, where directions remain to be established. The immediate 5 years will normally comprise commitments that have already been made.

## What if scenarios

Foresight enables a range of possibilities for the future to be imagined and explored. In the process it can reveal lines of investigation previously thought impractical and impossible. For example, the viability of major infrastructure investment through cost benefit and impact analyses. These are essentially "what if" scenarios that encourage radical or innovative questions to be asked and to be explored. Their value is to demonstrate that the future is not necessarily a projection of the past and present but an area to be explored and imagined. It enables answers found to the key question for all strategies. "What does better look like?" This is where a strategic Vision can play its part in raising expectations and showing clearly what could be possible when taking the long view.

## The precautionary approach

The visionary dimension to foresight will always be complemented by the precautionary approach, which looks at the impact, in social, economic and environmental terms, of visions and strategies and, in consequence, the nature of any risks involved.

# Subsidiarity – Who plans what?

## Effective governance - Decision making at the level to which it applies

An earlier chapter looked at Subsidiarity and who does what. A diagram set out the agenda for effective and integrated governance and planning at the national, regional and local levels. This chapter looks in detail at who plans what.

## The wider view from National government - Issues of national significance and National planning Frameworks

Governance at the National level is best placed to keep well informed about issues of global significance, such as Climate change, Biodiversity. Economic globalisation, Migration and Global transportation. It will often be participating in the global forums dealing with these issues. From this informed position it can help to set a wider context for Regional governance and planning in its National planning Framework. Such issues will also be on the agenda of a National Foresight group. In addition, National governance is best placed to initiate social, economic and environmental research into key issues of national significance.

## Decarbonisation and energy strategies

Decarbonisation and energy strategies would be expected to include clarification of the measures that should be taken, over what period, to achieve EU decarbonisation targets by 2030 and full decarbonisation by 2050, or as early as possible. Regional targets might be included. Measures to meet EU targets for the provision of renewable energy by 2030 and 2050, as a key aspect of decarbonisation, would also be included together with Regional targets

## Structural economic change

Any prospect of structural economic change* would be explained and its implications for Regions clarified, together with governmental support measures and programmes for transitional job creation, retraining and funding. A related issue will be any consequential rise in urban multiple deprivation and the need to also take this into account, on regional advice, in the provision of support funding.

\* See earlier - Globalisation and automation - The future of work. Automation and its impact on manufacturing and services

## Internal and external migration

Most migrational movement into and out of a country is generated by economic need, excluding consideration of refugee crises. However, refugee crises are expected to grow as the impact of global warming is increasingly felt in southern and equatorial countries. The appropriate response to environmental crises that generate flows of refugees is to mitigate these at source. As global warming intensifies this course of action may become impossible. In which case Europe will face a need for collective and "communitaire" action.

European countries have tended to be selective in their accommodation of migrants. It might be expected that National planning Frameworks will be clear about external migrational expectations both economically driven and crisis driven.

Internal migration, within the EU and nation states, may be difficult to quantify in either the medium or longer term. However, prospective skill shortages have, in the past, become apparent and met with incentives to prospective migrants. There is an ethical issue when skills flow from poorer to richer countries and it is clearly preferable for richer countries to meet their own skills needs. National planning Frameworks can clarify national intentions.

## National transportation networks and interchanges

National transportation networks, particularly high-speed rail, have a key role to play in equalising access to economic opportunities. They enable decentralisation and the development of regions. They enable a polycentric approach to the development of metropolitan regions. There is a clear European preference for high-speed train travel over short haul flights for journeys under 400 kilometres. The European high-speed train network is increasingly comprehensive in its cover and integration of services. A dedicated high-speed freight network is in the making.

In this context road travel may become a less attractive option for longer journeys but the move to Internet shopping is, of itself, generating increased local delivery flows. Whilst road congestion and its management may remain an issue, dealt with in city centres with congestion charging, the move to electric and hydrogen powered vehicles, and away from carbon fuel emissions, will make this less of an environmental issue.

National planning Frameworks might be expected to include consideration of the future roles of the strategic road, rail, air and shipping networks, their integration and programmes for their development in the medium and longer terms.

Well-integrated national transport networks have focussed on interchange as a key function. Shipping and container ports and airports integrated with strategic road and rail networks. Past rates of growth in containerisation will be unsustainable if the production of consumer goods moves closer to markets. The future of port and airport functions will be at the forefront of prospective economic change towards more sustainable, and decarbonised, lifestyles. This will also be a key strategic issue for National planning Frameworks.

## Urban rail connectivity

Urban Europe has inherited an extensive urban rail network, developed over the past hundred years or so with the coming of the industrial age, to carry passengers and goods of all kinds. It is a heavy gauge network designed for the locomotives of the past and their freight loads. They have provided an invaluable inheritance of routes that can be adapted to commuting uses with lighter and faster trains.

93

Their virtue is that, at their best, they can provide rapid transport to centres, with punctuality and comfort. However, commuting pressures have led to their becoming less reliable and over crowded, making car usage more attractive.

These circumstances might be expected to change with a growth of home working, speeded by COVID 19, and the automation of both production and services employment. Commuting peaks could decline and the capacity of rail services be used more for multi-purpose trips to centres, for example, for higher education, higher-end comparison retailing and entertainment.

As well as this radial urban connectivity a need has emerged for high-level connectivity to national and regional airports and ports. The nature of the urban flows to these could also be expected to change as the European high-speed train (HST) network becomes even more extensive, affecting airports, and global shipping in automated products declines and short sea shipping (SSS) increases, affecting ports. However, it might be expected that rail connectivity to airports, by HST and light rail or tram services from urban interchanges, will remain a necessity and that the need for dedicated rail freight services to ports will develop as SSS increases.

## Public services

Health, education and welfare services, provided on an integrated basis, form the foundation for a "communitaire" approach to wellbeing and quality of life. They can ensure equality of social and economic opportunity and promote social cohesion. As such they are the fundamentals of the good society.

However, they can be negated by poor housing conditions. Good housing that provides comfortable shelter to families and individuals is the base from which participation in urban social and economic life becomes possible. In Europe homelessness should not be an issue but is.

Europe also has an issue with multiple deprivation, where social and economic problems become compounded by a poor housing and a poor environment. National planning Frameworks might be expected to take a view on the need to tackle multiple deprivation and the resources and programmes that can be made available to do so.

## National environmental safeguarding

National environmental safeguarding would include aspects of the natural and built environment, including, for example, National Parks, strategic cycle networks and walkways, water catchment areas, areas of biodiversity interest and areas for heritage conservation. Such resources will frequently have global or European recognition.

## National and Regional Parks and tourism

National Parks have become established European institutions to safeguard areas of great beauty and natural interest and enable access to them on a managed basis. They were intended to respond to the pressures of increased mobility and tourism in a sustainable way. They have their counterparts at regional level in Regional Parks. Their use for recreation and enjoyment needs to be managed and sustained, usually through strategic planning, warden and ranger services.

Such parks are often areas of scientific and ecological significance, for example, in terms of their geology or habitats. Climate change will inevitability affect these natural resources and how they are sustained. Flora and fauna are on the move north and what are considered native species will change accordingly. National and Regional Parks will be at the forefront of the environmental changes that can be anticipated with climate change.

National and Regional Parks often come under pressure for the exploitation of their mineral resources, which may be unique or of great commercial value, their renewable energy resources, for example, for wind farms or hydro electric schemes and for commercial forestation. It has been a general strategic planning principle that National and Regional Parks should be designated, essentially, to safeguard them in their natural state and to protect them from development. This is a value judgement in the public interest that should not be undermined.

## Costal routes and long distance footpaths

National coastal routes and long distance footpaths are now well developed as a benign means of access to sensitive natural areas, particularly National and Regional parks. They can be integrated with routes and cycle routes at the regional level to enable comprehensive access to the countryside around metropolitan areas and to remoter rural areas. They can bring a form of tourism that is in sympathy with the conservation and safeguarding needs of sensitive areas. They can be economically significant to the rural areas of regions and metropolitan regions.

## Marine nature reserves and fish farming

More recently, awareness has increased of the value of comparable marine natural resources. Fish and shellfish farming has grown significantly and the "carrying capacity" of inland waters to absorb them, without environmental damage, has become an issue. Extensive Marine nature reserves have been designated to protect the most valuable inshore ecologies.

For the many metropolitan regions that are located on estuaries or the coast, the balance to be struck between the safeguarding and use of marine resources will be a strategic issue.

The regional, and metropolitan, view - Issues of regional significance and regional, and metropolitan, strategies

The regional and metropolitan region view will be informed by a National planning Framework and the global and national context and strategic guidance that it can provide. The regional agenda will be similar in some respects to the national agenda but will give specific policy and locational definition to it. The regional level is where the enabling process begins.

## Decarbonisation and renewable energy provision

The regional strategy will be able to define the specific measures to be taken to achieve EU decarbonisation targets. For example, how waste energy from buildings will be reduced, perhaps through a major programme of building insulation and the installation of electric heating powered by solar panels and thin film solar on buildings.

It will also be able to define locations for the provision of wind and solar farms, having regard to the most favoured areas for generation and their environmental acceptability. The regional strategy can also define locations for major forestry planting to assist the decarbonising process and, when mature, to provide a source of renewable energy. These will be the regionally significant measures.

They can be complemented by a range of additional urban measures including, for example, hydropower, tidal and river flow turbines, thermal power and storage, hydrogen based gas network supplies and heat pumps.

## Urbanisation

The regional level is where an informed judgement can be made about the capacity of a metropolitan region to recycle its land and buildings for new and alternative uses to meet the levels of need for urban development in prospect. Where the turnover of land and buildings (Brownfield) is insufficient then judgements can be made on the scale of land release required (Greenfield). In most cases this can be expected to be in peripheral urban locations that are well connected to the strategic transport network and have the least adverse environmental impact.

Consideration can be given to the creation of "Greenbelts" to contain future land release and protect farming and other rural functions around urban areas. The creation of a defensible urban edge, for example, through the planting of strategic tree belts will help to sustain the Greenbelt against arguments that it is degraded by its proximity to urban areas and should be developed. In effect, that it is no longer green.

## Renewal and regeneration priorities

There will be areas within a metropolitan urban area that have suffered from industrial decline, resulting in swathes or vacant and derelict land that may be polluted to a greater or lesser extent. Such land may have a negative value because of the cost of its restoration. Here public action to acquire and restore the land will be necessary, in the public interest. It can then be added to the regional brownfield land supply and help to meet future development needs. It may be that this is a more economic option than Greenfield development if it saves on new infrastructure costs.

In addition, in Europe, there are large urban areas of great heritage value and significance, which require protection and on-going conservation. They also will need definition, recognition and a programme of renewal and regeneration. The best form of conservation is the continued active use of the heritage building stock. A regional Strategy will be able to define, promote and resource a programme of urban renewal and regeneration focussing on vacant and derelict land and buildings and areas of heritage significance.

## Brownfield and Garden Festivals

One original and effective means of bringing major Brownfield sites, often vacant and derelict industrial land, forward for regeneration is the Garden Festival. It enables the physical restoration of the land, and the treatment of pollution, and its representation as a location of beauty and attraction rather than dereliction and decay. It is an effective measure available in support of a metropolitan region's strategy of renewal.

## Housing, industry, commerce and retailing need, demand and provision

These needs will be at the heart of any regional Strategy. There are proven strategic planning methodologies through which to make the strategic forecasts required and to roll these forward to maintain their realism and credibility (for example, see www.ssp7696.eu which contains an archive of the planning publications of the former Strathclyde Region, in Scotland).

For housing the methodology involves, in summary, assumptions and projections about demographic change, household formation, capacity of the existing building stock (public and private rental and owner occupied), tenure split (household preferences for rental or ownership) and consideration of land reuse (Brownfield) and release (Greenfield).

For industry and commerce the methodologies involve, in summary, an inventory of land and buildings and an assessment of their fitness for purpose and need for modernisation. A judgement of the strengths and weaknesses of the metropolitan economy and the prospective growth or decline of demand for premises.

For retailing the methodology involves, in summary, the definition of a hierarchy of shopping centres, of regional and local significance, and their catchment areas. An inventory of land and buildings, their size, floor space and retail turnover by centre. Forecasts of household expenditure in retail catchment areas on consumer durables and convenience goods and their growth prospects. Finally, a comparison of retail capacity with prospective retail expenditure by retail catchment area and centre and an assessment of the need for additional retail floor space or its rationalisation. The latter is becoming increasingly necessary with the rise of Internet retailing and services.

## Public service provision

The changing needs for health and education provision will be a function of the organisational arrangements for their delivery. These will reflect technological change. The implications for a regional Strategy will be a matter for corporate cooperation, having regard, for example, to any regional strategy for multiple deprivation priorities and regional land release.

## Centres

Centres matter. They are the focal points for community activity and multi-purpose trips and the maintenance of their vitality, viability and accessibility by public transport is a strategic issue. A regional Strategy will be able to identify all the development opportunities in the hierarchy of centres and bring these to the market. Such recognised opportunities will then be a defence against unjustified out of centre proposals. They will be key part of the enabling role of the regional Strategy.

## Regional transportation networks

These provide the structure for mobility in a region. Where the metropolitan region has a comprehensive rail or metro network then local bus services can feed into stations, interchanges and centres. It will help the functioning of the metropolitan area when renewal and regeneration areas, areas of multiple deprivation and areas of new development (Brownfield or Greenfield) can be linked into this network. Higher housing densities at nodal points on the network will also be supportive of a strategy of urban consolidation rather than extension.

Where a comprehensive rail network does not exist, or is not planned, then road space management to favour future electric or hydrogen buses will be appropriate. It has been mentioned earlier that accessibility on demand, from driverless electric vehicles, may have a future role to play in providing access to transport network nodes and interchanges. Commuting and peak hour congestion may decline with the rise of working from home. Working from home may generate more local journeys, which, again, may be provided for by accessibility on demand rather than car ownership.

## Regional green networks

The concept of metropolitan green networks has come to the fore with the increasing realisation that nature within urban areas functions best through connected parks, open spaces, areas of woodland, river valleys and areas of water, such as lakes or reservoirs. The development of biodiversity and a wide range of linked and related habitats is then possible. The importance of "green lungs" in urban areas is now more recognised, as global warming requires the cooling of the urban fabric.

## Regional environmental safeguarding

This function complements that at the national level. It enables the recognition of valued natural and heritage resources of regional significance and their safeguarding through protection, conservation and reuse as appropriate. It also enables their interpretation to promote greater understanding of their value.

## Infrastructure – Water and sewerage

Water supply and sewerage disposal are related issues that require planning and management at the regional level within defined water catchment areas.

Such planning will include the inter-related consideration of river systems, their capacity and environmental sensitivity, reservoirs and hydropower, flood management and water supply potential. Within urban areas there will be issues of surface water run off and wastewater treatment and disposal.

As a general rule water supply and sewerage services are taken as being capable of supporting Brownfield sites from existing urban networks and Greenfield sites from their extension. However, many of Europe's urban sewerage systems were laid down in much earlier times and are now in need to strategic renewal and replacement. Their capacity if often a major strategic issue and the cost of super collector sewers can be comparable to new metro systems. For example, the new UK Thames Tideway scheme, under the River Thames, is 35km long and will cost some £5bn.

In these circumstances such projects might be carried out through co-operation at national and regional levels of governance to plan their routes and fund their implementation. The private sector will also be involved if water and sewerage services have been privatised.

## Infrastructure - Telecommunications

Telecommunications have now become the critical support service through which urban life is sustained. They have moved from landline networks to satellite communications and support all aspects off modern life, including its domestic, social and economic dimensions. Technological change is taking place rapidly.

It is for these reasons that strategic planning for Telecommunications might be considered as key issue for the Foresight function discussed earlier. e-commerce, e-education and e-health and welfare are also discussed earlier as aspects of Globalisation and automation - The future of work.

## The local, and community, view - issues of local significance and local plans and proposals

The local and community view will have regard to the context provided by the regional Strategy, which will, predominantly, provide policies and programmes on the issues discussed above. The role of local planning will be to give locational definition to these through local Plans and proposals.

Local planning will also add the important dimension of local needs for housing, industry and commerce, retailing, public services, transportation and greening. It is at the local Plan level that public consultation is most meaningful. It is where communities can see the realities of the planning process, from national Frameworks, through regional Strategies to local Plans. There will then be a feedback loop to these other levels that may lead to a review of what is proposed. This is where the cycle of regular update and review of regional Strategies enables them to remain sensitive to local concerns.

## A subsidiarity spread sheet

The Subsidiarity spread sheet Good Governance - Effective Planning, at the end of the chapter Subsidiarity - Who does what, shows how an effective and integrated process of National, Regional and Local planning can work.

# The Metropolitan dimension – Where it all happens

## Urban Europe is primarily metropolitan - Where strategies become reality

There are 272 metropolitan regions in Europe, with populations over 250,000, and they comprise almost 70%, or some 300 million, of Europe's population of 448 million (Eurostat 2020). They are the locations where Europe's most pressing problems and opportunities materialise and where strategic planning can have its greatest effect in supporting Europe's wellbeing. They are, for this reason, the places where good governance and effective planning, through subsidiarity, can achieve the most.

The reality of urban Europe is of a dynamic mixture of vibrant city life, heritage and contrasting areas of deprivation and affluence. Added to this is the mix of cultures arising from Europe's colonial past. In times of prosperity all this can result in a celebration of multi-culturism but tensions have arisen when employment opportunities decline.

## Levelling Up - Good Governance and Effective Planning

As with many other areas of economic life, monopolies dominate city centre service industries such as banking and insurance. In times of financial crisis the whole structure of dependent support services, including those that have been out sourced, feels the effect. Social cohesion, an EU objective, has been difficult to sustain in such circumstances. The impact of the COVID 19 lockdowns, with many service providers working from home, has demonstrated these realities and their unemployment consequences, particularly for the hospitality industries.

In a globalised financial world, Europe's global cities, London (finance), Paris (tourism), and Madrid (the Spanish speaking world) have felt the impact of crises most strongly. Their planning problems and opportunities are in a different league from other metropolitan regions. The Paris metropolitan region is a European strategic planning exemplar.

The 27 EU national Capitals together include 80 million (Eurostat 2015), or some 30% of Europe's metropolitan population. They too have an international dimension to their life through their tourism attractions and their central governance and administrative functions. This has insulated them, to a degree, from global crises and their unemployment consequences. Central governance planning tends to focus on capital cities, which are seen as the shop windows for their country's way of life and success. They receive public finance accordingly and attract significant private investment interest.

The remaining regional capitals are more dependent on the well being of their areas of influence, or hinterlands, and the other metropolitan core cities that they are related to on a polycentric basis. Polycentricty is a European regional characteristic that lends strength to a region by adding diversity and inter-dependence to its economy.

This hierarchy of diverse and varied metropolitan regions and core cities gives Europe the unique urban characteristics that it has. With varied societies and economies with long histories and traditions and areas of great beauty. It is these special qualities that makes good governance and effective planning so necessary, to sustain them, and of such value.

## The many functions of centres - Accessibility and mixed uses

The definition of Europe's metropolitan regions by Eurostat is based on a core city and it's area of influence, that is, adjoining areas from which 60% of the population commute to the core. The original work by ESPON (European Spatial Observatory Network) considered the functions of the core that were relevant to its role and attraction. These included, in summary, administrative functions (governance, institutions and headquarters), decision functions (subsidiaries), knowledge functions (higher education, research and high technology production), tourism and cultural functions (congresses, fairs etc.) and transport functions (connectivity and interchange with other metropolitan regions).

Although such indicators were based on available data they do illustrate the inter-related functions that influence the overall attraction of a metropolitan region and its core city, or polycentric cities. In strategic planning terms this results in centres that are strong because of their mixed uses, including housing (apartments, student accommodation etc.).

## Land use and transportation - Mobility and connectivity

The core functions of metropolitan regions are what generate the major transportation flows to them. They are sustained by good transportation connections and interchanges. Connectivity, to other metropolitan regions and beyond, grows by all modes of transport, as the metropolitan region grows. However, the importance of such connectivity is changing as the COVID 19 pandemic has revealed the potential to work and meet on-line. It has revealed essential and non-essential communications and when, and when not, face-to-face meetings are required. The pandemic has also revealed the true nature of the "soft" power of metropolitan core cities in enabling and facilitating the informal face-to-face exchange of knowledge and ideas that has always been the fundamental attraction of cities through the ages.

In the digital age the traditional relationship between land uses and the urban movements they generate has changed. Mobility and connectivity now embrace consideration of the relative need for physical and digital connectivity as broadband speed becomes as important as transportation speed and journey times. The result may be structural changes in the way the metropolitan transport system functions as commuting and radial movement to the core diminishes and local movement increases around the periphery and between polycentric centres. This can be seen as a response to the prospective decentralisation of office functions and their related support functions.

# The idea of greening - Environmental quality and the multiple benefits of nature

One of the great attractions of European cities is their compact nature, with many opportunities for social inter-action within walking distance. The urban fabric of buildings, streets and public spaces gives all cities their unique character and sense of place. But these qualities are complemented by their green networks of parks, river banks, walkways and cycle ways often linking beyond the urban area to the surrounding green belt or to regional resources such as forests, nature reserves and country parks.

This wider strategic framework of linked habitats adds to the character and attraction of cities. It requires recognition, protection and conservation through planning.

# What might better look like?

## A Citizens Dividend - A return on the nation's social capital - a universal basic income - the "Portfolio" economy

The purpose of society is to enable citizens and families to lead happy and fulfilling lives. Fulfilment can happen through the arts, public services or business, through family life or the many opportunities presented by urban life. Society should offer support in times of distress. This is the "communitaire" approach, which recognises the uncertainties of life and the support that is required in times of need.

Support through the provision of health, education and welfare services provides part of the answer, together with a transport system that provides affordable access to employment opportunities. However, as has been discussed in earlier chapters, the nature of full-time, secure, well-paid employment is changing. How to earn a living in the future has become much less certain.

The concept of a Citizens Dividend has arisen in response to these uncertainties. It recognises that all citizens contribute to the social capital of society (its services, institutions and businesses) over their lifetimes and that a Citizens Dividend is a payment on this investment. It removes the idea of state benefits as unearned charity.

The objective of a Citizens Dividend is to remove the lack of a basic living income as the greatest cause of stress and breakdown in society. It is a means of supporting social cohesion and reducing social disparities. It would provide a basis from which to stabilise life in the "portfolio economy" where household income may come from a number of sources, including the market economy, public employment, self employment and on line businesses, involving all members of an extended family.

A universal Citizens Dividend would also address the problem of the bureaucracy often involved in claiming state benefits. These tend to target benefits selectively depending on personal or family circumstances. They require claimant's knowledge and understanding of what can be a complex process. The result is often low take up and continued hardship.

## An end to poverty and homelessness

The great blight on European life, within some of the richest countries in the world, is continuing poverty, particularly child poverty, and homelessness. Good governance and effective planning has a role to play in alleviating this, through the identification of areas of multiple deprivation, but there does also need to be recognition that the private sector housing market will not fulfil the need for low cost rental housing. Affordability, even with the underlying support of a Citizens Dividend, means housing built at cost on land where a development premium has not been paid. Brownfield sites, with negative value, restored at public cost would be one source of such land.

## Life long learning - Beginning in the nursery

Children are best placed to benefit from their primary education when they have enjoyed the benefits of nursery education and an early introduction to the communication skills required to benefit from primary education. To be able to talk and socialise using an extended vocabulary. Primary schooling often has to employ remedial measures in the early years. This is one important indicator of multiple deprivation.

As the prospects for pensions become more uncertain, through low returns on investments and diminishing cohorts of younger employees contributing, a Citizens Dividend would become more relevant to older generations. Life long learning is a concept that recognises that skills need to be sustained, and new skills acquired, throughout a lifetime. And even more so in the portfolio economy. All this needs strategic planning.

## Health security

After basic universal income security, health will be the greatest concern for families and individuals, especially when they become vulnerable in old age.

The COVID 19 pandemic has illustrated that there is no substitute for an effective public health service to meet all health needs as they arise. Health is a function of a healthy lifestyle, which those living on low incomes or state benefits cannot always afford. There is a public interest in universal health as a function of the good society. Good governance and effective planning have a role to play.

# Climate security - Global warming mitigated and stabilised

Society needs confidence that the international, national and regional action being taken to avert dangerous global warming will prove to be effective. Citizens can then take personal responsibility for how they behave in the knowledge that this will contribute to strategies for climate change mitigation that are going to work. The world needs to feel that it is on course to keep the earth habitable for humanity. Climate change is an inter-generational issue where present generations need to recognise their responsibilities to future generations and the children of today. Good governance and effective planning for decarbonisation will be essential for success.

## Biodiversity security - Species loss stopped

The global loss of biodiversity is as great a threat to humanity as climate change. Metropolitan areas need inventories of their natural resources and their inter-relationships in order to consider how best to sustain them. The green networks of metropolitan urban areas, when they connect the full range of corridors, open spaces, parks, rivers and woodlands, provide the range of habitats necessary to support biodiversity. The natural functions of the network need to be recognised, understood, safeguarded and fostered with the support of good governance and effective planning.

## Environmental recovery - The damage of the past, to urban quality and natural resources, recovered

The de-industrialisation of many of Europe's metropolitan regions has left its mark in terms of vacant and unused land, dereliction and pollution. This has often been compounded by more recent structural technological change in industries such as chemical production and energy generation. The recovery of such Brownfield sites and their recycling and reuse may be on a scale requiring strategic recognition. Such recovery may release development or environmental opportunities. For example, there is a thriving movement of Garden Festivals in Germany, which, as well as opening up opportunities for new land uses, changes the perception of an area from negative to positive.

## The index of human happiness - High scores across Europe

The World Happiness Report (WHR) is published annually by the United Nations Sustainable Development Solutions Network. It ranks countries by available data on a number of key indicators where data is available from published sources or representative survey. The current indicators are GDP per capita, social support, health and life expectancy, freedom to make life choices, generosity and perceptions of corruption. They confirm the importance of the factors that it is concluded make for happy and fulfilling lives in metropolitan regions, namely, freedom from worry about income, and effective public support services, particularly health, welfare and education.

**The WHR finds, not surprisingly, that cities within high scoring countries also rank highly. It would seem to indicate that good governance, at national and regional levels, is key factor in generating wellbeing and its resulting happiness.**

# Exemplars – Europe does it better

## German governance

Germany is a federal parliamentary republic with power vested in the state parliament (Bundestag) and the representative body of the sixteen regional states (Bundesrat). In 2016 the Bundesrat produced the equivalent of a national planning Framework (Concepts and Strategies for Spatial Development in Germany). The issues covered, below, show the context that the national level in Germany provides for the regional states and the concerns of national significance that it would expect to see reflected in regional Strategies.

**It demonstrates the value that Europe's strongest national economy sees in the function of strategic planning and of the concept of subsidiarity for good governance to enhance competitiveness, ensure provision of public services, control and sustainably develop land use, shape climate change and transform the energy system.**

# Concepts and Strategies for Spatial Development in Germany

### *Enhance competitiveness*

- *Evolve metropolitan regions*
- *Strengthen cooperation and the interlinking of areas*
- *Support areas with a special structural need for action*
- *Ensure infrastructural links and mobility*

### *Ensure the provision of public services*

- *Consistently apply the central places system*
- *Develop cooperative systems*
- *Ensure the supply of sparsely populated rural areas*
- *Ensure accessibility*

### *Control and sustainably develop land uses*

- *Minimize spatial conflicts of use*
- *Create large-scale open space networks*
- *Shaping cultural landscapes*
- *Reduce new land take*

- *Sustainably control the use of mineral resources and other subterranean uses*
- *Sustainably use coasts and seas*

**Shape climate change and the transformation of the energy system**

- *Adapt spatial structures to climate change*
- *Control the development of renewable energy and of networks*

## Dutch spatial planning

Amsterdam Metropolitan Areas (AMA) comprises a partnership of 33 municipalities. It has adopted the following Agenda (2016-2020) for its Strategic planning, which covers and confirms many of the key issues raised in Levelling Up.

- *Provide space for living and working (how should the region develop spatially?)*
- *Smarter and more innovative working (how can the regional tech economy be strengthened?)*
- *Improving quality of life (how will we ensure that the cities, villages and landscape in the region remain attractive?)*

- *Accelerating the transition to a clean economy (what concrete steps need to be taken towards a fossil-free and circular regional economy?)*

- *Improved connections (how can regional accessibility be improved and maintained?)*

- *Making the metropolitan region climate-proof (how do we ensure sufficient water storage and collection capacity?)*

- *Making the metropolitan region more agile (how can regional decision-making respond more quickly to new developments?)*

**The City of Amsterdam Structural Vision (2011) looks to 2040. The following extracts from the Foreword corroborate much of the approach advocated in Levelling Up and exemplify subsidiarity in practice at the metropolitan region and city levels.**

- *The Structural Vision is a framework of analysis for spatial plans and provides the basis for setting the city's investment agendas, but first and foremost the Structural Vision is a visionary scenario for the future.*

- *In the Structural Vision, Amsterdam City Council sets out its ambitions for the period 2010 to 2040.*

- *Amsterdam has deliberately opted for densification of the city centre. The city has not chosen for growth by increasing its*

127

*surface area but for intensification of the existing urban territory and for transformation of business zones.*

- *By building 70,000 new dwellings with accompanying amenities within the city's existing boundaries we can expand the city centre milieu that makes the city so attractive.*

- *That is only feasible if we simultaneously invest in the public space, public transport and greenery.*

- *People want to live in Amsterdam because of its combination of metropolitan bustle and large expanses of greenery within a short distance of each other. That is our strength, with which we draw in residents and business enterprises.*

- *In the Structural Vision, Amsterdam emphatically looks beyond its borders. Problems, challenges and opportunities present themselves on the scale of the Amsterdam Metropolitan Area, so the Vision Map covers the whole territory between Zandvoort, Purmerend, Almere and Haarlemmermeer.*

- *This is the region that must operate as an economically robust entity on the European and international stage, in order to be able to compete with, for example, the Ruhr Area. Amsterdam is the core city within this region and its showpiece.*

- *The Structural Vision outlines the ambition for the long term, which is why the vision must be continuously readjusted in the light of current events, such as the economic crisis.*

- *Or, indeed, quite the contrary: in turbulent times, the vision for the future must provide a framework of analysis to determine the plans that ought to be executed and those that are of secondary importance.*

- *The vision for the future should not be swayed by the issues of the day; it must map out how we respond to them. Only then can Amsterdam become both economically strong and sustainable.*

*Maarten van Poelgeest*
*Alderman for Spatial Planning*


# UK - The Scottish experience

Glasgow and the Clyde Valley once featured almost at the bottom of the EU rankings of urban deprivation. A review of governance in Scotland* concluded that local government needed to be reformed to create strong metropolitan regions and regional authorities, with the full range of powers necessary to address deprivation and urban decay in the comprehensive and integrated

129

**way that was necessary. They needed to be effective at a time of urban crisis.**

Eight Regional Councils were set up, one of which, Strathclyde Regional Council, covered the metropolitan region of Glasgow and the Clyde Valley. This included 1.8 million (2016) or about 33% of Scotland's population of 5.5million (2019). It was given powers of strategic planning, transportation planning and provision, education and welfare provision and planning and police and fire services. Health remained a function of Scottish central government, through regional Health Boards, and public sector housing a function of local District Councils.

Scotland's Regional Councils existed for twenty years, from 1976 to 1996, until the Scottish Parliament was set up. During its lifetime Strathclyde was the biggest local authority in the UK and much of Europe. Its achievements demonstrated the length of time that it takes to change the realities and perception of deprived and degraded metropolitan regions. Twenty years were needed before the marketing slogan "Glasgow's Miles Better" became a reality universally recognised. It had a strong corporate and physical planning capability and its Structure Plan was give the first European Award for Regional Planning in 1990/1991.

Only now is the UK, following it experience of COVID 19 and the need to act regionally, beginning to consider the need for good regional governance in England. The experience of the good governance of regions and effective strategic planning in Scotland will provide an exemplar.

The essence of its success was an ability to address multiple deprivation with integrated public service and environmental recovery, including the renewal and regeneration of housing and vacant and derelict land. It used its strategic planning powers to change the direction of urban development away from Greenfield release, including New Towns taking Glasgow population "overspill", and back towards the reuse and recycling of Brownfield sites. Related to this was a strong defence of centres and the putting in to practice of greening and green networks. The extensive existing rail and metro systems were sustained.

**The Scottish experience, from long strategic practice, confirms the value of an holistic approach to metropolitan governance and of a synoptic view of the strategic planning of regions.**

A web site has been created (www.ssp7696.eu) to hold, for reference, the full range of key strategic planning documents produced by

Strathclyde Regional Council (SRC), including the Strathclyde Structure Plan. A reprint of the then ground-breaking Clyde Valley Regional Plan of 1949, produced by Patrick Abercrombie and Robert Matthew, was published by SRC in 1996 .

A postscript to the Scottish experience is that after Regional Councils were disbanded in 1996 their strategic planning functions, through the Structure Plan process, were continued by the successor metropolitan local Councils through Joint Committees. These are the local planning authorities and they were given the statutory power to plan strategically but only is they acted collectively.

**This recognised the value of effective metropolitan region planning and adopted a unique strategic planning power sharing formula for its continuation. It is a model that might have wider European application where a formal additional regional or metropolitan tier of governance is not practical.**

\* Royal Commission on Local Government in Scotland 1975, called the Wheatley Report.

# We need planners - Educating the planners

## Planners and the public interest

The function of good governance and effective strategic planning is to reflect the public interest in a whole range of related social, economic and environmental issues and to take an integrated and synoptic view of them, as a basis for forward planning for the medium and longer term. Levelling Up has explored these to promote awareness of what is needed in planning education and practice. How to educate the planners that society needs?

## Planners are the ultimate generalists - Insight and relationships

Because of the range of inter-related issues involved in good governance and effective planning, planners need to be the ultimate generalists. They need to have a working knowledge and understanding of the issues they will face and their inter-related nature. For example, as the exemplar of Germany shows, for social solidarity and cohesion as the basis for a competitive economy.

133

# Levelling Up - Good Governance and Effective Planning

It is for this reason that Universities are best placed to provide the range of insight needed. It means planners sitting in on the foundation courses for many disciplines and these disciplines themselves providing direct inputs into planning courses. This holistic approach to planning education can give graduates the broad base of knowledge, understanding and insight they will need in their professional lives as advisers to good governance at the national, regional and local levels.

There are, of course, areas of expertise that are specific to planning, such as the modelling of catchment and market areas for housing, retailing and transportation, of environmental networks and environmental impact and of the conception, preparation and communication of visions, scenarios, strategies and plans.

Public consultation on all of these requires clarity of thought and the "reasoned justification" that is mandatory for all levels of planning. The planning triumvirate of "survey, analysis, plan" has remained valid, in principle, over the years although now more complex, as is society itself.

Above all, clarity about where the public interest lies, and then what is in the public interest, is a planning and political matter. In a mixed economy, such as the Europe of the European Union, provision by the market and the public sector, separately or in partnership, is the norm. This means that what is in the public interest may, on occasions, also be in the interests of the market. For example, as the exemplar of Germany shows, social strength is economic strength.

Politics, at all levels of governance, is a noble calling when it seeks to address the complexities of life, and "what might better look like", in the public interest and in an holistic way rather than with sectoral or special interests in mind. Planning can contribute most when governance is good. Planning education can provide the generalist skills needed to provide the informed advice that good governance needs.

## Specialisation is for postgraduates

It will be in the nature of things that planning graduates will develop particular interests during their courses and become curious about, and engaged with, particular issues. Planning needs specialists to do in depth research and to take the body of planning knowledge further. For example, in the whole area of planning data handling and modelling. Models have a mixed reputation because they have sometimes been wrongly taken as predictions rather than insight into possibilities and the means of exploring the consequences of "what if" scenarios. They are tools for thinking not a substitute for it.

Planning should always be open to graduates from particular related disciplines, such as the social sciences, to take up planning through postgraduate courses. As Levelling Up hopefully shows, there are many skills required to contribute to informed planning at all levels. It should be possible to go from generalist to specialist and specialist to generalist. Postgraduate courses in planning would enable this.

## Experience and qualification

As with all professions, a degree of experience is required to add practice to education leading to qualification. Professions have been seen as "closed shops" but planning is, by its nature, open, all embracing, and "communitaire". As Patrick Geddes has said, "To plan is a basic human need" and it involves having an understanding of humanity in all its complexities. Experience adds reality to theory. Qualification endorses education and practice and confirms "fitness for purpose". Respect follows from effectiveness.

**Levelling Up provides an indication of the key issues that might be covered in graduate planning courses at Universities.**

# Communitaire – The politics of basic human needs

## The Atlantic and the European socio-economic models

There are, essentially, two schools of Western thought about the good society and how to achieve it. One might be thought of as the Atlantic model, which is economically and socially competitive with a social safety net. It is essentially a meritocracy. The other might be thought of as the European model, which is economically and socially "communitaire", or cooperative, within a welfare state that aims to level up opportunities and reduce disparities.

In the Atlantic model education is a competitive process leading to the selection of the successful for employment and the widening of social disparities. In the European model it is assumed that society is at its most successful, socially and economically, when all have the opportunity from education to realise their potential and social disparities are mitigated. Social cohesion is seen as an economic good providing the social capital that all can benefit from as stakeholders in society.

137

There is also the "mixed economy" that combines aspects of both models and works on the basis of cooperation between the public and private sectors in economic development, for example, through partnerships involving infrastructure and development, and the provision of social services, for example, through public and private schools, universities and hospitals.

National, regional and local governance will be required in all these circumstances but the process of strategic planning, offering enabling foresight, will differ in each from the indicative to the more specific. The role for planning in all of these models will be to define and enable the public interest.

## The public interest is common interests

There are some issues that can only be addressed at particular levels of governance. This is the concept of subsidiarity. It is also the concept of the public interest at each level. Without good governance at each level, and particularly the level of the metropolitan region where such a high percentage of Europe's population lives, citizens are disenfranchised from some of the crucial strategic decisions that will affect their wellbeing in the future. Such as provision for liveable and affordable housing in locations with good accessibility to centres, public services and public transport.

In a mixed economy there are bound to be tensions between profit driven motives and public interest motives. They can be the same thing, as with partnerships to diversify and strengthen a regional or local economy, but they can also be at odds, as with the wish of monopolies to minimise competition or when they have a severe impact on the vitality and viability of centres.

Good governance and effective planning enable the public interest to be given definition, quantitatively and locationally, and for this to be expressed positively, through planning strategies to enable development that supports the public interest and meets demand for development from markets. For example, by identifying, defining and marketing all the retail development opportunities in the centres of a metropolitan region in order to positively enable their take up before consideration is given to of out of centre locations. This would require regional and local planning to work together.

## Some things can only be achieved collectively

Good governance and effective planning is an act of collective will, taken in the public interest in working towards "what might better look like". A key aspect is the process of public consultation, built into most planning legislation, which requires complete transparency about data and information, how it used, the process of decision making involved and how it is informed. They key wording, as always, is "reasoned justification".

It is not just a question of having an informed electorate but of an electorate that recognises that foresight is helpful in giving insight into possible futures and that deciding almost invariably means choosing. Visions and strategies
only have worth when an electorate is supportive and appreciates the need for a "communitaire" approach to make them reality.

## Achieving better - Communitaire politics

Communitaire politics are essentially cooperative rather than confrontational. They recognise that, almost invariably, there is much more that communities have in common than there are differences. Communitaire politics seeks to keep this common ground always in focus and to make judgements based on their implications for a supported Vision or Strategy. Strategic planning is, by its nature, a communitaire activity.

# How to make it happen – Who needs to do what?

## Governance and subsidiarity

Nation states need to look critically at their governance and to review this on the basis of subsidiarity and the need to establish levels of governance that reflect the need for collective action on the issues that can only be addressed effectively at each level. This is the basis of good governance.

It will then provide the platform, at each level, for effective planning. This, in turn, and over the medium and longer term, will be able to demonstrate the value of informed foresight to help to identify and realise possibilities for the future, that is, "What might better look like?"

## Visions and reasoned argument

To make such Visions reality they will have to be based on reasoned argument. On argument that is well founded on fact and probability. The concept of "reasoned justification" should be the basis for effective planning at all levels. Where the necessary information is not available then it will have to be gathered, over time. It will always be necessary to make judgements based on the best information available but it will also be necessary to recognise where there are gaps in this and to remedy them. Planning is a rolling process of update and review and time enables it to become better informed.

## Planning as enabling

Without good governance at the national, regional and local levels, planning will be seen as a controlling rather than an enabling process. The critical level is the region and metropolitan region. Without effective strategic planning at this level, there is a danger that the necessary decisions will be taken at the national level with strategic decision making becoming more and more centralised. Planning at the local level is left without the strategic enabling context it needs and is faced with exercising judgements, and control, on a local reactive basis.

## A voice for planning

Where good governance does not exist at the regional or metropolitan region level planning does not have a voice. There cannot be an appreciation of its value as a means through which to realise better futures.

Everyone has plans, whether it is for the future of their family or themselves. As Patrick Geddes has said "To plan is a basic human need". What all communities do not have, and what they could have, is "communitaire" based plans for their collective future wellbeing. For "What might better look like".

**Fundamentally, it is only Good Governance and Effective Planning that can present the possibilities and, over time, help to realise them.**

# Appendix 1

# Detailed chapter summaries by paragraph

## What happened? – How planning lost its way

- Centralisation
- Loss of regional and local autonomy
- Monopolies
- Planning as controller rather than enabler
- Short term versus long term - The electoral cycle
- The market for planning – Meeting basic human needs
- Reasoned justification - Informed decision making
- What happened? – How planning lost its way

## Subsidiarity – Who does what?

- Subsidiarity - The idea of context and a hierarchy of integrated rolling decision making
- Central government - The wider context

- Regional and metropolitan government - The planning strategies
- Local government - The operational plans of local policies and proposals
- How subsidiarity makes for good governance and effective planning
- Complexity - Defining Regions

## The big forces for change – The wider context

- Global warming and environmental impact
- The world post COVID
- Globalisation and automation
- The financialisation of everything

## Global warming and environmental impact - Migration and biodiversity

- Mitigation - Stabilising climate change
- Urban energy saving and renewable energy generation
- Urban mobility - Commuting and the need to travel

- The hydrogen economy - Feedstock, storage and source of power
- Transportation - Goods and tourism - Aviation and Shipping
- Transportation - Road and rail
- Sustainable food supplies

## The world post COVID – How the need for change became obvious

- Governance and COVID 19
- Austerity and financial resources
- Pandemic management - Lessons for regional planning
- Deprivation and disparities
- Health inequalities
- Housing inequalities
- Employment and income inequalities
- Education inequalities
- Health services and caring
- Working from home - Internet shopping
- Subsidiarity becomes operational - Integrated national, regional and local action
- Some conclusions

## Globalisation and automation - The future of work

- Globalisation - Labour costs and transportation
- Automation and its impact on manufacturing and services
- The Portfolio economy - Employment and occupations
- A Citizens Dividend - universal basic income
- Taxation and public expenditure
- Pensions
- Self sufficiency and sustainability
- Regional and local economies
- e-commerce, e-education and e-health and welfare
- Artificial Intelligence (AI)

## The financialisation of everything - Development as an asset

- Financialisation
- Consumption and global warming
- Interest rates, investment and asset values
- Development pressures and speculation
- Housing and inflation - Ownership as an asset
- Housing affordability - The need for a rental sector

- Capital and disparities

## What needs planning – The really important issues

- Housing need - The relationships between housing market areas, migration, household formation and tenure
- Economic mobility and change - The new regional economies
- Centres matter - Changing roles and the future of retailing
- Mobility and transportation - Changing patterns of traffic generation
- Safeguarding what we value - The built and natural environment

## The synoptic view – How the pieces fit together

- The synoptic view
- A strategic vision - Where are we trying to get to?
- Foresight and what is probable or possible
- Planning as an integrated rolling process
- Variable rates of change and the need for updates and review

## Foresight – Taking the long view

- Directions, probabilities and possibilities
- What if scenarios
- The precautionary approach

## Subsidiarity – Who plans what?

- Effective governance - Decision making at the level to which it applies
- The wider view from National government - Issues of national significance and National planning Frameworks

  Decarbonisation and energy strategies

  Structural economic change

  Internal and external migration

  National transportation networks and interchanges

  Urban rail connectivity

  Public services

  National environmental safeguarding

  National and Regional Parks and tourism

  Costal routes and long distance footpaths

  Marine nature reserves and fish farming

- The regional, and metropolitan, view - Issues of regional significance and regional, and metropolitan, strategies

  Decarbonisation and renewable energy provision

  Urbanisation

  Renewal and regeneration priorities

  Brownfield and Garden Festivals

  Housing, industry, commerce and retailing need, demand and provision

  Public service provision

  Centres

  Regional transportation networks

  Regional green networks

  Regional environmental safeguarding

  Infrastructure - Water and sewerage

  Infrastructure - Telecommunications

- The local, and community, view - issues of local significance and local plans and proposals
- A subsidiarity spread sheet

## The Metropolitan dimension – Where it all happens

- Urban Europe is primarily metropolitan - Where strategies become reality
- The many functions of centres - Accessibility and mixed uses
- Land use and transportation - Mobility and connectivity
- The idea of greening - Environmental quality and the multiple benefits of nature

## What might better look like?

- A Citizens Dividend - A return on the nation's social capital - a universal basic income - the "Portfolio" economy
- An end to poverty and homelessness
- Life long learning - Beginning in the nursery
- Health security
- Climate security - Global warming mitigated and stabilised
- Biodiversity security - Species loss stopped
- Environmental recovery - The damage of the past, to urban quality and natural resources, recovered
- The index of human happiness - High scores across Europe

## Exemplars – Europe does it better

- German governance
- Dutch spatial planning
- UK - The Scottish experience

## We need planners - Educating the planners

- Planners and the public interest
- Planners are the ultimate generalists - Insight and relationships
- Specialisation is for post graduates
- Experience and qualification

## Communitaire – The politics of basic human needs

- The Atlantic and the European socio-economic models
- The public interest is common interests
- Some things can only be achieved collectively
- Achieving better - Communitaire politics

## How to make it happen – Who needs to do what?

- Governance and subsidiarity
- Visions and reasoned argument
- Planning as enabling
- A voice for planning

# Appendix 2

## Europe's 272 Metropolitan Regions

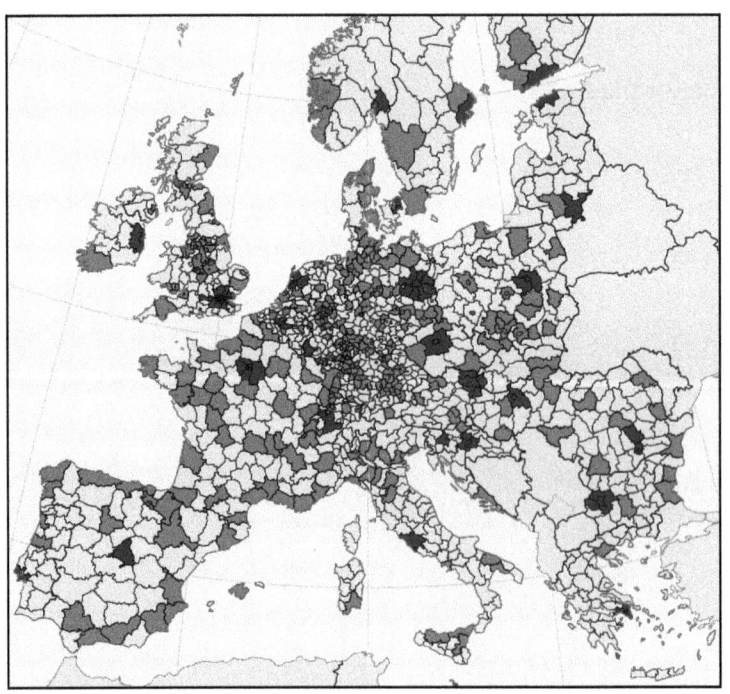

© Eurostat

## Levelling Up - Good Governance and Effective Planning

This diagram by Eurostat is of Europe's 272 Nuts 3 (Nomenclature of Territorial Units for Statistics) areas, or Metropolitan Regions, with populations over 250,000. It illustrates their widespread distribution and geographic and territorial significance.

**They are the missing dimension to governance in many EU countries.**

# Acknowledgements

The following are some of the books have been influential in providing the insight that Levelling Up has drawn on.

- The meaning of the 21st Century -James Martin
- 10 billion - Stephen Emmott
- The hot topic - Gabrielle Walker and Sir David King
- Cancel the apocalypse - Andrew Simms
- A final warning - James Lovelock
- Storms of my grandchildren - James Hansen
- Project sunshine - Steve McKevitt and Tony Ryan
- How we can save the planet - Mayer Hillman
- The suicidal planet - Mayer Hillman with Tina Fawcett and Sudhir Chella Rajan
- Heat - George Monbiot
- The switch - Chris Goodall
- Ten technologies to save the world - Chris Goodall
- Sustainability - All that matters - Chris Goodall
- What We Need To Do Now - Chris Goodall
- How much is enough - Robert and Edward Skidelsky
- Humans need not apply - Jerry Kaplan

# Levelling Up - Good Governance and Effective Planning

- The zero marginal cost society - Jeremy Rifkind

- The third industrial revolution - Jeremy Rifkind

- The end of work - Jeremy Rifkind

- Prosperity without growth - Tim Jackson

- Automation and the Future of Work - Aaron Benanav

- A World Without Work - Daniel Susskind

- Globalisation and its discontents -Joseph Stiglitz

- Post Capitalism - A guide to our future - Paul Mason

- Stolen - How to save the world from financialisation - Grace Blakeley

- Smart Cities After COVID 19 - Ten Narratives - Klaus R. Kunzmann

- European data, analysis and insight in many fields - Eurostat

# Biography

Roger Read trained as an architect and added town planning in the 1960's when there was still a mass of work in post war urban renewal and with New Towns. He eventually became Deputy Chief Planner for Irvine New Town, in Scotland, and then Deputy Director of Physical Planning for Strathclyde Regional Council.

When Strathclyde was dissolved in 1996, with the advent of the Scottish Parliament, he founded, with others, METREX, the Network of European Metropolitan Regions and Areas and became its first Secretary General.

He has, therefore, spent some 50 years thinking about planning and the multitude of considerations that are involved. He has written METROPOLITAN - The Lost Dimension, which was published in 2018.

© Roger Read

# Is European Governance fit for purpose?

**It is hoped that this book will be of interest to all those with a concern for public affairs, be they politicians, officials, advisers or citizens.**

- Has **Subsidiarity** become established as the guiding principle of **Good Governance**, that is, that Issues should be tackled at the level to which they apply? For example, at national, regional, metropolitan (city region) or local levels.

- And is there **Effective Governance**, the capability to take decisions in the public interest based on well-informed and reasoned argument, at each of these levels?

- And is the need for **Foresight** recognised, looking to the medium term of 5- 10/15 years, where strategic issues are clear but decisions have yet to be taken, and to the longer term, from 15-25/30 years, where choices remain to be made?

- And is the need for a **Synoptic View** of the future recognised, that sees that all strategic issues are inter related and need a coherent approach to their resolution?

- And is there a **Strategic Planning** capability, at all levels, which enables scenarios of the future to be explored, choices to be identified, decisions to be taken in the public interest and then put into effect through Good Governance and Effective Planning?

**Read Levelling Up, if these are issues that interest you.**

Lightning Source UK Ltd.
Milton Keynes UK
UKHW022309170122
397287UK00007B/1476